getting a handle on
WORSHIP

Exploring Its Meaning • Responding in Simplicity

Whaid Guscott Rose
Israel Steinmetz

Getting a Handle on Worship
by Whaid Guscott Rose and Israel Steinmetz

Published by Vibrant Church Initiatives.
Cover and interior design by Rick Frye.

ISBN 978-0-9972689-0-4

CONTENTS

PREFACE

Writing another book on worship is sort of like writing another worship song. One wonders, *Is it really necessary?* With so many others that have come before, why do we need one more? Like the great hymns of the past, other books on worship are more comprehensive, more theologically rich, and more beautifully written than what we could offer. Past songs and books express eternal truths that need not be restated or reimagined. So why contribute something more to the vast collection of worship?

The answer for writing another book on worship is the same as the answer for writing another worship song: No matter how many songs or books are written, we can never exhaust the topic. We are finite creatures sharing glimpses of an infinite God. Every generation must rise up and sing new songs to the God who reveals Himself anew in every generation. And every one of us must reflect on the glory of God and the part we play in bringing Him glory. A. W. Tozer's charge that "We must never rest until everything inside us worships God"[1] is a challenge we must all embrace with all we are.

So, here are some glimpses of what it means to worship God, offered by two men who have committed not to rest until everything inside us worships God. Or, to put it in Paul's words, "To do everything to the glory of God." We spent the two years leading up to the writing of this book touring the continent, teaching on the topic of worship, and joining brothers and sisters in the act itself. The lessons we taught along the way, as well as those learned over many years of walking with the Lord, are gathered here as a resource for the body of Christ to offer itself in worship. We hope to say something about worship that is both deeply theological and decidedly practical. We hope to put a tool in the hands of those who have committed themselves to worshipping God. This book is an offering of love to God and a gift to those who love to worship God and desire to explore worship's deeper meaning.

The ordering of the chapters, therefore, follows a pattern. We begin by establishing that we were created for worship, that worship is (or should be) our highest priority, and that this central place and role of worship in the economy of the kingdom is highlighted by a "worship thread" that runs throughout Scripture. Attention is then given to the development of a working definition of worship, showing that there's more to it than is commonly understood. To go deeper, chapters on the theology of worship and how worship has been viewed and practiced throughout Christian history come next. At this point, some of the practical aspects of worship are addressed, such as the role of music, designing dynamic worship services, and finding balance between traditional and contemporary, thereby lessening the worship wars that detract from worship's true purpose. The ending chapters take us back to the heart of worship, providing a biblical guide to making worship a matter of the heart and showing a picture of the worship of heaven as a model for worship here on earth. And as a bonus, additional thoughts are shared on worship etiquette (in the appendix), offering helpful suggestions (reminders) regarding acceptable and unacceptable behaviors in worship.

The layout of the individual chapters also follows a pattern. To help readers glean the most from these pages, the Big Idea and learning objectives are stated up front. It is hoped that reading each chapter with the central thought and objectives for takeaway in clear focus will increase the potential gain. The Big Idea is further reinforced with helpful quotes and applicable Scripture references. And there's more. Each lesson is concluded with questions for study and reflection. This format is intentional, designed to make this book a practical tool for exploring the meaning of worship. The chapters that follow are not just to be read for information. They are to be contemplated and digested, and to cause deep stirring in our hearts. It is to that end that these added elements are included.

Even so, the volume you hold in your hand is by no means an exhaustive treatment of the subject, but is rather, a sincere attempt to put a handle on worship so believers can get a hold on it for themselves. It is a humble attempt to address "the one thing that affects everything," a tool with which to explore the deeper meaning of a subject that affects all believers in one way or another. As you do, may the lessons and principles you discover prompt you to respond in simple faith, making your whole life an offering of worship to the Lord. This is the purpose for which we were created. This is how we "glorify God and enjoy him forever."[2] This is the sincere hope and grand aim of this volume. Thank you for reading it.

Endnotes

1. A. W. Tozer, as quoted by LaMar Boschman at http://lamarboschman.com/10-great-quotes-on-worship/. Web accessed 10-14-15.
2. Taken from the Westminster Shorter Catechism, http://www.creeds.net/Westminster/shorter_catechism. html. Web accessed 10-14-15.

ACKNOWLEDGMENTS

Our heartfelt "thank you" to the team of individuals whose various contributions, including crafting learning objectives and review questions, copyright research, seemingly endless manuscript editing, and book layout, make this volume a reality: Amber Riggs, Sherri Langton, Hope Dais, and Rick Frye.

Thanks to Heber Vega for heading translation efforts to make this book available in Spanish.

Thanks to the members of our faith community across the US and Canada, whose growing interest in this subject and participation in the Worship in the Spirit Conference Tour provided much impetus for the completion of this book project.

Thanks to our wives, Marjolene (Whaid) and Anna (Israel), and families, for allowing us the freedom of time to devote to this effort, time that would otherwise have been spent with them.

Thanks to our Lord and Savior, Jesus Christ, without whom we would have nothing to write about.

ABOUT THIS BOOK

T his book is designed to be a practical study tool for individuals and groups. The following features in each chapter are intended to help you better understand and apply the content:

The Big Idea, as identified by the "light bulb" icon, is a brief synopsis of the key thoughts and central theme for each chapter. After reading the chapter, review the Big Idea to help galvanize the central theme in your mind.

The objectives are identified by the "target" icon and indicate skills you'll develop as a result of reading the chapter. You'll have an opportunity to practice these skills in the Review Questions at the end of the chapter.

The "book" icon precedes quotes and scriptures that capture the chapter's key ideas in a memorable way. Consider committing one or more of the quotes or scriptures to memory.

Sidebars help to highlight important thoughts or supplemental materials. Don't skip over them!

The review questions are designed to help you remember what you've just read. The application questions help you to put what you've read into practice. Consider discussing the questions with a friend or small group.

While you have the option of simply reading this book, the best way to *Get a Handle on Worship* will be to utilize these tools to help you understand, remember and apply what you've read. May God bless you as you seek to worship Him!

CHAPTER 1

CREATED TO WORSHIP

Worship is universal in its appeal and practice. All peoples and cultures worship. We can't help ourselves; it's part of our DNA. We were created by God for the purpose of worship. As one writer puts it, we will therefore either worship the true God or we will worship an idol, but worship we must.

After reading this chapter, you will be able to

- identify the purpose for which human beings were created;
- identify the unique qualities of human worship;
- define *idolatry*.

And when those beasts give glory and honor and thanks to him that sat on the throne, who lives for ever and ever, the four and twenty elders fall down before him that sat on the throne, and worship him that liveth for ever and ever, and cast

their crowns before the throne, saying, Thou art worthy, O Lord, to receive glory and honour and power: for thou hast created all things, and for thy pleasure they are and were created (Revelation 4:9–11, KJV).

Question: "What is the chief end of man?" Answer: "Man's chief end is to glorify God, and to enjoy him for ever."[1]

Thou hast formed us for Thyself, and our hearts are restless till they find rest in Thee.

— Augustine, Bishop of Hippo

There is a God-shaped vacuum in the heart of every man which cannot be filled by any created thing, but only by God, the Creator, made known through Jesus.

— Blaise Pascal

———————————————

Who am I? Why am I here? What is life really all about? These questions reflect the quest of humans to discover life's true meaning and purpose. And attempts to answer them have given rise to various ideologies and world religions. But within the biblical and Christian worldview, a very simple and straightforward answer is offered.

The Westminster Shorter Catechism begins with this question: "What is the chief end of man?" The answer: "Man's chief end is to glorify God, and to enjoy him forever."

According to the catechism, the purpose for which humans were created is to glorify and enjoy God. This answer is based on the well-known biblical truth that we were created in the image and glory of God and therefore should do everything we do for God's glory. Consider the following scriptures:

> Then God said, "Let Us make man in Our image, according to Our like-ness; let them have dominion over the fish of the sea, over the birds of the air, and over the cattle, over all the earth and over every creeping thing that creeps on the earth." So God created man in His own image; in the image of God He created him; male and female He created them (Genesis 1:26, 27).

I will say to the north, "Give them up!"
And to the south, "Do not keep them back!"
Bring My sons from afar,
And My daughters from the ends of the earth—
Everyone who is called by My name,
Whom I have created for My glory;
I have formed him, yes, I have made him (Isaiah 43:6, 7).

For you were bought at a price; therefore glorify God in your body and in your spirit, which are God's (1 Corinthians 6:20).

Therefore, whether you eat or drink, or whatever you do, do all to the glory of God (1 Corinthians 10:31).

This answer offered by the catechism also finds support in some of the most noted quotations from the pages of Christian history and theology. Prime examples include the prayer of the fourth century theologian and bishop of North Africa, Augustine, and the 17th century Renaissance scientist and theologian, Blaise Pascal. Augustine prayed, "Thou hast formed us for Thyself, and our hearts are restless till they find rest in Thee." Pascal wrote, "There is a God-shaped vacuum in the heart of every man which cannot be filled by any created thing, but only by God, the Creator, made known through Jesus."

Augustine knew of what he prayed, for he spent a significant portion of his life in excessive indulgence in sensual pleasure before his dramatic conversion. His restless heart finally came to find rest in the only place where such rest can be found: in our Creator. And writing from the perspective of a scientist and theologian during the Age of Enlightenment, that period of influential thinkers in Europe and the new America that gave rise to a time of unique spiritual darkness, Pascal made the astute observation that separation from God caused a hole in our soul, and try as we may, the only cure for our dilemma is God himself.

But the catechism, Augustine, and Pascal merely echo a foundational truth of Scripture about God's design and purpose in the way in which He created us. God created the world and everything in it for "the praise of His glory," a phrase often repeated in Scripture, particularly in the New Testament. "All Thy works shall praise Thy name in earth and sky and sea," declares the hymn writer. Psalm 104 is a song of praise to God motivated by the sheer wonder of what He has made. God created the universe because it expresses His glory. "The heavens declare the glory of God," David writes in Psalm 19. In Psalm 148 God's creation (the natural world) praises Him in recognition of His infinite wisdom and might. But notice that by the end of this psalm praises rise, not from the sun, moon, and stars, but from the lips of humanity:

> Kings of the earth and all peoples;
> Princes and all judges of the earth;
> Both young men and maidens;
> Old men and children.
>
> Let them praise the name of the Lord,
> For His name alone is exalted;
> His glory is above the earth and heaven.
> And He has exalted the horn of His people,
> The praise of all His saints —
> Of the children of Israel,
> A people near to Him. (Psalm 148:11–14)

PRAISE THE LORD!

God created everything for His glory, but He is particularly interested in the glory that comes from those made in His own image ("the imago dei") and given the special privilege of a personal relationship with Him. Nothing in God's creative order is able to praise Him in the way in which we humans can. In his book, *The Reward of Worship: The Joy of Fellowship with a Personal God*, Pastor Jack Hayford notes that

> Human beings stand apart from all other creatures by the gifts of self-initiated speech and song bestowed only upon us. By creative capacity, our tongues are able to speak and to sing; no other creature can do that. We may speak of birds singing, but as lovely as that is, birdsong is not consciously generated singing....Only humankind creates new songs and links them to consciously created lyrics that express more than a mere animal response of a natural endowment.[2]

We see therefore that our unique capacity for worship is by design; by making us in His image, God placed in us an intrinsic capacity for worship. Because of our intrinsic capacity for worship, we will either worship the true

God or worship an idol. That's why the human heart is given to idolatry, why we are "Prone to wander...Prone to leave the God I love,"[3] why we tend to worship whatever is in front of us, why Adam and Eve yielded to the Devil's temptation. An idol is whatever substitutes for God, whatever we believe can be and do for us what only God can be and do. This is Paul's point in the opening chapters of Romans: "because, although they knew God, they did not glorify Him as God, nor were thankful, but became futile in their thoughts, and their foolish hearts were darkened. Professing to be wise, they became fools, and changed the glory of the incorruptible God into an image made like corruptible man—and birds and four-footed animals and creeping things" (Romans 1:21–23).

This truth, that we were created for God's glory and pleasure, gives meaning and purpose to our lives. It is a reminder that we are not the result of some chance collision of molecules, but rather, the crown jewels of God's creation, formed and fashioned in His image and after His likeness. We began with Him, and though it seems that some are moving away from Him, He is our destiny. We are created for Him, and we are indeed restless until we find our rest in Him. We are created for worship.

> Humanity has always been on a quest to discover life's true meaning and purpose. That is likely the reason Rick Warren's book, *The Purpose Driven Life*, has turned out to be one of the best-selling Christian books of all time—called "a runaway best-seller." Why have so many millions bought Warren's book? No doubt because it addresses a deep human need—the quest for meaning and purpose. And according to Warren, the secret to discovering our purpose is making God the reference point of our lives.

REVIEW QUESTIONS

1. What is the purpose for which we were created?

2. What is unique about human worship?

3. What is idolatry? Why is the human heart given to idolatry?

APPLICATION QUESTIONS

1. Imagine you have walked into a room full of people, and you scan the room to see who is enjoying themselves. What signs do you look for to tell you if people are enjoying something or someone? What are some internal signs of enjoyment that you may not be able to see?

2. Based on the internal and external signs of enjoyment that you just iden-tified, when do you currently enjoy God the most?

3. List five ways in which humans give God pleasure.

4. How are you currently giving God pleasure?

5. What are three areas in which you struggle to keep God "in front of" you?

6. What are three ways in which you can consciously keep God "in front of" you?

Endnotes

Scripture quotations are from the *New King James Version* unless otherwise noted.

1. *The Westminster Shorter Catechism*, http://www.creeds.net/Westminster/shorter_catechism.html. Web accessed 10-14-15.
2. Jack Hayford, *The Reward of Worship: The Joy of Fellowship with a Personal God* (Grand Rapids: Chosen Books, 2007), 130.
3. Robert Robinson, "Come, Thou Fount of Every Blessing"

CHAPTER 2

THE PRIORITY OF WORSHIP

Worship is a whole lot more than a once-a-week activity. As our chief end and God's grand purpose in creating us, worship is to be the church's chief priority. It should be that which informs everything else that the church is and does.

After reading this chapter, you will be able to

- identify the church's highest priority;
- understand how worship gives meaning to the other purposes of the church;
- explain the relationship between worship and evangelism.

And every creature which is in heaven and on the earth and under the earth and such as are in the sea, and all that are in them, I heard saying:

"Blessing and honor and glory and power
Be to Him who sits on the throne,
And to the Lamb, forever and ever!"

Then the four living creatures said, "Amen!" And the twenty-four elders fell down and worshiped Him who lives forever and ever" (Revelation 5:13, 14).

Christian worship is the most momentous, the most urgent, the most glorious action that can take place in human life.[1]

Joy [God in us] is the serious business of heaven.[2]

Love that goes upward is worship; love that goes outward is affection; love that stoops is grace.[3]

O ne of the essentials of a healthy church is the setting of clear priorities. Its members know what's most important, what the biblical purpose of the church is. In fact, a healthy church will have multiple priorities based on multiple purposes.

That's why so many have come to embrace the purposes of the church set forth in Rick Warren's bestselling book *The Purpose Driven Church*. For the benefit of those who are unfamiliar with this material, these purposes are worship, service, evangelism, fellowship, and discipleship. They are drawn from what Warren calls the two great scriptures of the Bible: 1) the Great Commandment in Matthew 22:34–40 (which is based on the Shema in Deuteronomy 6) and 2) the Great Commission in Matthew 28:19, 20. As Warren asserts, a church that gives attention to the Great Commandment and the Great Commission will be a great church.

Suffice to say, the first two purposes (worship and service) are drawn from the Great Commission, and the last three (evangelism, fellowship and discipleship) are drawn from the Great Commandment.

The Great Commission

And Jesus came and spoke to them, saying, "All authority has been given to Me in heaven and on earth. Go therefore and make disciples of all the nations, baptizing them in the name of the Father and of the Son and of the Holy Spirit, teaching them to observe all things that I have commanded you; and lo, I am with you always, even to the end of the age" (Matthew 28:18–20).

The Great Commandment

Jesus said to him, "'You shall love the Lord your God with all your heart, with all your soul, and with all your mind.' This is the first and great commandment. And the second is like it: 'You shall love your neighbor as yourself.' On these two commandments hang all the Law and the Prophets" (Matthew 22:37–40).

A healthy church knows what its priorities are, but it also has a chief priority or purpose—one that ranks higher in importance, one that informs the others. So the question is: What should be the highest priority or purpose of the church? To what should the church give closest attention and devote its greatest resources? Of the five purposes, which one should stand out above the others?

A common response to the above question is evangelism. That response is understandable given much emphasis of the Great Commission—and for good reason. After all, this was the last command uttered from the lips of the resurrected Christ prior to His ascension, and that alone gives it importance. That's why it isn't called the Great Suggestion, but rather, the Great Commission. However, while the Bible places great importance on reaching the lost, a comprehensive look at Scripture shows that worship, not evangelism, is to be the church's highest priority. Effective evangelism must be preceded by effective worship, for it is worship that gives substance and meaning to evangelism and the other purposes. Jesus told Martha in Luke 10:42 that the best service flows out of a worshipping heart, "Mary has chosen the better part." In other words, void of biblical worship, service becomes drudgery, and fellowship is reduced to a social gathering. In the final analysis, it is worship that informs all that the church is called to be and do, which is the reason the Father seeks worshippers, not workers (John 4:23, 24). Don't miss Jesus' important counsel to Martha in Luke 10:42: Our work can distract our worship, but our worship enhances our work.

Becoming true worshippers is the pathway to becoming true disciples. When we find ourselves needing more hours in our day to fulfill life's many demands, we must be all the more determined to make room in our day for worship—that which should fuel everything else that we do. The German reformer Martin Luther well understood this principle. He was known to spend the first four hours of his day in private devotion. When counseled by his associates to cut back on his devotional time to accommodate his busy schedule, he reasoned that all the things he had to do in a given day made it all the more important to devote extended time with the Lord. Prayer and personal devotion, regular time alone with God in worship, should be our highest priority, both as individuals, and as a church.

Better yet, we should see all that we do throughout our day as worship. We are admonished by Paul to do everything we do to the glory of God, including eating and drinking (1 Corinthians 10:31). *Our work is worship.* Even the mundane activities of our daily routine are to be viewed as worship. Indeed, worship is the highest priority of the Christian life. So let us therefore consider some of the biblical principles that form the basis for this assertion:

1. **We were created for the purpose of worship (Revelation 4:11).** Worship should be our highest priority, because it is the purpose for which we were created. This is the beginning point of making the case for the priority of worship.
2. **Worship is first and foremost about God (Exodus 20:1–2).** The opening lines of the Ten Commandments—God's identity and His command to have no other gods before Him—point us to the grand object of our worship: God Himself.
3. **Jesus commends worship, underscoring its importance to a dynamic relationship with Him (Luke 10:42).** Jesus placed a high premium on worship by commending Mary for choosing "the better part." What was "better" about her choice is that it demonstrated her understanding of the priority of worship, its critical importance to a dynamic relationship with God.

4. **Worship is the ultimate goal of our redemption (1Peter 2:9), and will be the preoccupation of eternity (Revelation 5:8-14).** The goal of redemption is worship, to show forth the praises of Him who called us out of the darkness of sin into the light of His love. Worship now is therefore preparation for the ceaseless worship of eternity.

5. **Experiencing the fullness of the Holy Spirit is directly linked to our capacity to honor God with biblical worship (Ephesians 5:18-19).** One of the key New Testament admonitions to be filled with the Spirit is given in the broader context of an admonition to sing psalms, hymns and spiritual songs, linking Spirit fullness and worship.

6. **The Father seeks worshippers, not workers (John 4:21-24).** Our work matters to God, but it is possible for our work to push God to the periphery of our lives, the reason God seeks worshippers instead, the kind who will make Him the serious business of their whole lives.

7. **Worship is key to spiritual victory (2 Chronicles 20), evangelism (John 3:14-15), and fervency (Acts 2:46-47).** Judah defeated the enemy in battle, not with weapons of war, but by appointing a choir; Jesus promised that if we lift Him up (which, in our context, is worship) He will draw the masses to Himself, and the secret or fuel of the early church's spiritual fervor was its passion for the worship of God. Worship isn't perfunctory to all the other important things the church does. It is the one thing that affects everything.

The goal of this chapter is to provide convincing evidence from Scripture that as our chief end and God's grand purpose for our lives, worship is to be the highest priority of the church, or at least should be..

MISSIONS AND WORSHIP

Therefore, as a fitting conclusion to this chapter, we call your attention to the following quote by Dr. John Piper. Be careful not to stumble over the second sentence: "Missions exist because worship doesn't." You will stumble over it if you think of worship as something we do once per week. Piper is using the word worship in a much broader sense—as our chief end, to glorify God in everything we do, and to enjoy Him forever. In other words, the reason we do missions is because humanity has forsaken its chief and purpose. That's why missions exist—because worship doesn't, because not all humans are living out the purpose for which they were created. Here is how Piper puts it:

THE SUPREMACY OF GOD IN MISSIONS THROUGH WORSHIP

Missions is not the ultimate goal of the church. Worship is. Missions exists because worship doesn't. Worship is ultimate, not missions, because God is ultimate, not man. When this age is over, and the countless millions of the redeemed fall on their faces before the throne of God, missions will be no more. It is a temporary necessity. But worship abides forever.

Worship, therefore, is the fuel and goal of missions. It's the goal of missions because in missions we simply aim to bring the nations into the white-hot enjoyment of God's glory. The goal of missions is the gladness of the peoples in the greatness of God. "The Lord reigns, let the earth rejoice; let the many coastlands be glad!" (Ps. 97:1). "Let the peoples praise you, O God; let all the peoples praise you! Let the nations be glad and sing for joy!" (Ps. 67:3–4).

But worship is also the fuel of missions. Passion for God in worship precedes the offer of God in preaching. You can't commend what you don't cherish. Missionaries will never call out, "Let the nations be glad!" if they cannot say from the heart, "I rejoice in the Lord...I will be glad and exult in you, I will sing praise to your name, O Most High" (Pss. 104:34; 9:2). Missions begins and ends in worship.[4]

Essentially, Piper's point is that worship takes priority over everything else because worship is about God, who should be our ultimate priority, the worship of whom will be the priority of eternity, where everything will narrow down to one thing—the ceaseless worship of the Lamb upon His throne. Such will be our highest priority then. Why not make it our highest priority now?

REVIEW QUESTIONS

1. What is the church's chief priority? Why is this to be the highest priority of Christian life?

2. How does worship give meaning to the other purposes of the church?

3. Why is there a need for missions? Why does it exist?

APPLICATION QUESTIONS

1. How does worship fuel each of the priorities of the church and of Christian life?

2. Is it possible for the other purposes of the church to distract from worship? How?

3. What is the relationship between time alone with God in worship and living out your day as an act of worship?

4. What are the most "mundane activities" of your daily routine? How can these be transformed into acts of worship?

5. Does worship as the chief purpose of humans cause you to approach evangelism differently? How?

Endnotes

Scripture quotations are from the *New King James Version*.

1. Karl Barth, quoted in *The Worship of God* (Grand Rapids: Wm. B. Eerdmans Publishing Co, 1982), 1.
2. C. S. Lewis, quoted at http://www.goodreads.com/quotes/67336-joy-is-the-serious-business-of-heaven. Web accessed 9-11-15.

3. Donald Grey Barnhouse, quoted in Grace Restoration Ministries (http://gracerestoration.org/grace-that-stoops/). Web accessed 9-1-15

4. John Piper, *Let the Nations Be Glad! The Supremacy of God in Missions* (Grand Rapids: Baker Academic, 2010), 35–36.

CHAPTER 3

SCRIPTURE'S WORSHIP THREAD

Worship isn't incidental to the Scriptures. There's a clear "worship thread" that runs throughout, from beginning to end, from Genesis to Revelation. This sheds light on the priority of worship in the heart and mind of God, and how that priority should affect the way we worship.

After reading this chapter, you will be able to

- identify the beginning of the worship thread in Scripture;
- identify ten ways in which worship is expressed in the worship thread;
- describe the future of worship as it is foreshadowed in Revelation.

"You search the Scriptures, for in them you think you have eternal life; and these are they which testify of Me. But you are not willing to come to Me that you may have life" (John 5:39, 40).

———————————

As mentioned previously, worship isn't incidental to the Scriptures; it is foundational to it. This is beautifully highlighted by what is called a "worship thread" that runs through the Bible from beginning to end. This sheds light on the priority of worship and how that priority should affect the way we worship.

It's a long thread, so not every part of it will be highlighted in this lesson. But we'll see enough of it to know that it's there and that it ties together the one thing that affects everything: worship.

CREATION *JOB 38:1–7*

It should not come as a surprise that the beginning point of this thread is at creation. Nothing is said in the early chapters of Genesis to indicate that worship happened as God spoke the world and everything in it into existence. Yet, such a commentary is found, of all places, in the book of Job. Caught in the vortex of his own grief, Job had been venting about God's failure to do something about his situation. So God challenged Job with a series of pressing questions too lofty for the human mind. The context of verse seven is creation, and the question is basically this: Where were you when the morning stars sang together, and all the sons of God shouted for joy? The obvious point is that even before there was a human voice, the stars and planets, accompanied by the angels (sons of God), sang to the God of creation in praise of His power and glory. This is the beginning point of the worship thread.

THE FIRST FAMILY *GENESIS 4:1–8*

Soon after creation and the establishment of the human family, even without any known instructions from God about worship, Cain and Abel offered sacrifices of worship to God. Worship was innate to their very nature. Makes sense, because we were created for worship.

THE ALTARS OF GENESIS

Each time Abraham encountered God in a special way (whenever God revealed Himself to Abraham) he marked the experience by erecting an altar. They're called spiritual markers, tracking Abraham's incredible walk of faith with God, beginning in Genesis 12. The rest of the book of Genesis is punctuated with these altars of worship, which highlights the worship thread in the book of beginnings.

THE TABERNACLE OF EXODUS

Exodus, the name of the second book in the Old Testament, literally means "exit," highlighting God's miraculous deliverance of the children of Israel from Egyptian bondage. But in terms of content, the real focus of the book is what they were brought out of Egypt to do, which is illustrated by the book's two main emphases: the giving of the law and the revelation of the pattern for the tabernacle of worship. God made His agenda clear at the burning bush—His purpose for bringing Israel out of Egypt was worship (see Exodus 3:12). Newer translations substitute the word *serve* for *worship*, which is one and the same. In fact, as we will explore in greater detail in a later lesson, Israel's encounter with God at Mount Sinai is more about worship than anything else, for more chapters in Exodus are devoted to the tabernacle than to the law. Thus, the Bible's worship thread can be vividly seen in Exodus.

THE PRIESTHOOD AND LITURGY OF LEVITICUS

For many Christians, reading through the book of Leviticus has become synonymous with an effort in boredom. Its meticulous details can be a challenge until the reader comes to see the book as an instruction manual on worship. The passion of Leviticus is the holiness of God, hence the repeated sentence, "For I am God; I am holy." The holiness of God demands that the worship of Him be adorned by holiness, the reason that early in the book Nadab and Abihu are killed for offering "strange fire" as acceptable worship to God (Leviticus 10).

So Leviticus is really a worship manual, not only for the Old Testament priesthood in ordering the worship of the tabernacle, but for New Testament Christians who, by applying its principles, may order the worship of their heart and life, the spiritual tabernacle in which God now dwells through the Holy Spirit. The worship thread seen here in Leviticus runs throughout the rest of the Pentateuch.

WORSHIP IN THE HISTORICAL BOOKS

The books that follow the Pentateuch (Joshua through Esther) are known as the historical books because they chronicle the history of God's people after the death of Moses and the crossing of the Jordan into Canaan through the rise of the four kingdoms prophesied in Daniel. Trying to see the worship thread in such a large piece of the biblical canvas is both daunting and intriguing. But we see it most prominently as the nation comes of age and demands a king. After the death of Saul, God brings to the throne of Israel "a man after His own heart." To be a man or woman after God's own heart is to be a worshipper, which is what David was at the very core of his being. It is therefore no surprise that his first great passion was to bring the ark of the covenant (which symbolized the very presence of God) back to Jerusalem. His second great passion was to build a permanent temple for the worship of God, a dream later fulfilled by Solomon, making the temple in Jerusalem the centerpiece of Jewish life and culture. So central was the temple to the life of the Jews that it became the focus of the invading kings and their armies, which carried away its artifacts, and later destroyed it. That's why the rebuilding of the Jerusalem temple is the big focus as we near the end of this section of the Old Testament (in Ezra and Nehemiah). Worship was central to the life of the nation of Israel, as these historical books show.

THE SONGS OF THE PSALMS

In the Hebrew language, the term *Psalms*, that body of scriptures in the middle of our Bible, literally means "praises," or "book of praises," affirming that this collection of "praise songs" was in fact the official hymnbook of the Hebrew people. Its prominent place in the liturgical life of the nation of Israel is paralleled by its special place in the lives of New Testament Christians. Indeed, we all love the Psalms. We love the Psalms because they give expression to the full range of our human emotions and experiences. They teach us how to settle our souls in the presence of God, how to be honest with God about our disappointments and doubts, how to tell God those things otherwise thought inappropriate, how to be joyful in praise, blessing the Lord with all that is within us. The Psalms teach us the priority of worship and prayer as pathways to a deeper and more intimate relationship with God. This portion of Scriptures' worship thread glistens with color and beauty, for "truly the light is sweet" (Ecclesiastes 11:7) and "You will show me the path of life; in Your presence is fullness of joy; at Your right hand are pleasures forevermore" (Psalm 16:11).

Consider the following verses from the Psalms on worship and love for the house of the Lord:

> But as for me, I will come into Your house in the multitude of
>   Your mercy;
> In fear of You I will worship toward Your holy temple (Psalm 5:7).

> Praise is awaiting You, O God, in Zion;
> And to You the vow shall be performed.
> O You who hear prayer,
> To You all flesh will come....

> Blessed is the man You choose,
> And cause to approach You,
> That he may dwell in Your courts.
> We shall be satisfied with the goodness of Your house,
> Of Your holy temple (Psalm 65:1, 2, 4).

> Oh come, let us sing to the Lord!
> Let us shout joyfully to the Rock of our salvation.
> Let us come before His presence with thanksgiving;
> Let us shout joyfully to Him with psalms....

> Oh come, let us worship and bow down;
> Let us kneel before the Lord our Maker.
> For He is our God,
> And we are the people of His pasture,
> And the sheep of His hand (Psalm 95:1, 2, 6, 7).

THE MAJOR AND MINOR PROPHETS

Some of the richest and most instructional Scripture passages on worship are found in the major and minor prophets. "These people honor me with their lips, but their hearts are far from me," one of the most oft repeated verses on empty and meaningless worship, is a quote from the book of Isaiah (29:13). So is the great throne room vision in which Isaiah sees the Lord, high and lifted up (6:1–8). We often repeat what's called the Micah Mandate ("He has shown you, O man, what is good; and what does the Lord require of you, but to do justly, to love mercy, and to walk humbly with your God?") without taking note of its context (Micah 6:6, 7). Its focus is worship: "With what shall I come before the Lord, and bow myself before the High God? Shall I come before Him with burnt offerings, with calves a year old? Will the Lord be pleased with thousands of rams, ten thousand rivers of oil? Shall I give my firstborn for my transgression, the fruit of my body for the sin of my soul?" And all serious worshippers should contemplate these poignant words in Malachi 1:10: "'Who is there even among you who would shut the doors, so that you would not kindle fire on My altar in vain? I have no pleasure in you,' says the Lord of hosts, 'Nor will I accept an offering from your hands.' Basically, God is wishing that someone would shut the door and turn out the light in the house of God so the people won't be able to offer insincere sacrifices. God would rather have no worship at all than worthless worship. This is strong language, but it shows the prominence of the worship thread in this section of the Old Testament.

THE GOSPELS

It is difficult to imagine what stark silence for 400 years between the prophecy of Malachi and the writing of the New Testament must have been like. There was no word or revelation from God for four centuries. The silence was broken by the announcement of the angel that the baby Jesus was to be born in Bethlehem, and the books of Matthew, Mark, Luke, and John (the four Gospels) give us an account of Jesus' birth, life, ministry, death and resurrection. It's the greatest story ever told about the greatest life ever lived. And the song by the heavenly hosts that accompanies the angel's announcement of Jesus' birth exposes Scripture's worship thread at the very beginning of these books (Luke 2:13, 14): "And suddenly there was with the angel a multitude of the heavenly host praising God and saying: 'Glory to God in the highest, and on earth peace, goodwill toward men!'" This song of the angels is joined by all the songs inspired by the life of Jesus for the past 2,000-plus years. As someone once said, He has indeed "furnished the theme for more songs than all songwriters combined." The worship thread of Scripture runs through the Gospels.

But in the Gospels we also see Jesus' passion to restore true worship as He cleanses the temple, as He confronts the religious leaders about their hypocrisy, and as He exercises power over nature, sickness and disease, demons, and even death. This is proof of His deity and raises the question every generation of God's people must ask and answer: "Who is Jesus and how do we relate to Him?" Our answer to that question will make all the difference in our personal lives and in the corporate worship of the church. We worship Jesus because He is God, the centerpiece of our worship. He is the reason we sing. The devil hates the song and thought he had silenced it when Jesus hung dead on the cross and lay in the grave. But that was only a rest note on the musical score of Jesus' song. The song didn't stop; it never will.

WORSHIP IN THE EARLY CHURCH

It's been said that "The Christian Church was born in song."[1] This statement may be considered conjecture, but if it's true, it points to the premium placed on worship in God's economy. What we do know for sure is that the New Testament church was born during the time of the annual Pentecost celebration. This Hebrew festival had long anticipated the coming of the Holy Spirit to indwell God's people. Now the disciples were gathered in the upper room to wait for the Spirit's arrival as Jesus instructed (Acts 1:4, 5). And it happened: The Spirit came upon them "like a mighty rushing wind" (Acts 2:1–4), launching the greatest spiritual movement in the history of the world. This happened during a prayer meeting that turned into an incredibly dynamic experience in the presence of God. Worship therefore becomes the hallmark of this new movement, as seen throughout the book of Acts.

One can easily miss this because the early believers had no regimens and patterns in worship such as we have today—no prominent sanctuaries or auditoriums, no well-equipped fellowship halls, and no vestibules in which to greet one another. The Jewish system of worship was still in place, so the early Christians needed to forge a new path of worship centered on the living Christ. Worship was therefore simple and integrated into all of life. It was a lifestyle: "So continuing daily with one accord in the temple, and breaking bread from house to house, they ate their food with gladness and simplicity of heart, praising God and having favor with all the people. And the Lord added to the church daily those who were being saved" (Acts 2:46, 47). Scripture's worship thread now takes on new shape and dimension as the worship of these early believers flows fresh and in pristine form out of hearts fixed on the risen Lord Jesus Christ, out of lives empowered and animated by the Holy Spirit.

WORSHIP IN THE EPISTLES OF PAUL

The simple lifestyle of worship seen in the early church in Acts now develops into established worship forms and patterns that have served as a guide for Christian worship in the centuries that have followed. Because Paul penned a significant number of the New Testament epistles and played such a major role in the establishment of the early church, his letters to the churches he planted is a good place to look for Scripture's worship thread in this section of Scripture. So consider these references:

> Rejoice always, pray without ceasing, in everything give thanks; for this is the will of God in Christ Jesus for you. Do not quench the Spirit. Do not despise prophecies (1 Thessalonians 5:16–20).

> ...speaking to one another in psalms and hymns and spiritual songs, singing and making melody in your heart to the Lord....(Ephesians 5:19).

> And let the peace of God rule in your hearts, to which also you were called in one body; and be thankful. Let the word of Christ dwell in you richly in all wisdom, teaching and admonishing one another in psalms and hymns and spiritual songs, singing with grace in your hearts to the Lord (Colossians 3:15, 16).

Other references could be cited, including Paul's instructions to the Corinthian church on how the gifts of the Spirit are to be manifested so that the order and beauty of worship can be preserved (see 1 Corinthians 14:40). But essentially, this piece of the worship thread portrays the church as a worshipping community, and that these earliest Christians developed their congregations around worship as a core value.

WORSHIP IN THE BOOK OF REVELATION

In his book *The Reward of Worship: The Joy of Fellowship with a Personal God*, Pastor Jack Hayford makes this astute observation about worship in the book of Revelation:

> Worship is the core value of the book of Revelation, whatever else is made of its prophetic pictures. No book of the Bible has had more written about it than this one, but too little notice has been made regarding the way it is laced through with scenes of worship.[2]

Indeed, the book of Revelation is more about worship than anything else. In a sermon years ago, Dr. Steven Lawson described the worship of Revelation as "worship at its best; worship that pleases God."

That is our aim—worship that pleases God—and how appropriate that we're given glimpses of such worship in the last book of the Bible. Here Scripture's worship thread blends into the sunlight of God's glorious presence, as it will be for all eternity.

IN SUMMARY

From the altars of Genesis to the throne room of Revelation, there's a thread that underscores worship's central place in Scripture, and thus, its central place in the economy of the kingdom, in the heart and mind of God. It gives credence to the principles at the heart of the two previous chapters: We were created for worship, and worship is to be our highest priority. This thread is a reminder that worship is foundational to Scripture, not incidental to it. Like the Jesus thread that runs throughout the Bible, it serves to keep us on course, focused on the one thing that affects everything.

NAME ABOVE ALL NAMES

In Genesis, Jesus is the Ram at Abraham's altar.
In Exodus, He is the Passover Lamb.

In Leviticus, He is the High Priest.

In Numbers, He is the Cloud by day and Pillar of Fire by night.

In Deuteronomy, He is the City of our Refuge.

In Joshua, He is the Scarlet Thread out Rahab's window.

In Judges, He is our Judge.

In Ruth, He is our Kinsman Redeemer.

In 1 and 2 Samuel, He is our Trusted Prophet.

In Kings and Chronicles, He is our Reigning King.

In Ezra, He is our Faithful Scribe.

In Nehemiah, He is the Rebuilder of everything that is broken.

In Esther, He is the Mordecai sitting faithful at the gate.

In Job, He is our Redeemer that ever lives.

In Psalms, He is my Shepherd I shall not want.

In Proverbs and Ecclesiastes, He is our Wisdom.

In the Song of Solomon, He is the Beautiful Bridegroom.

In Isaiah, He is the Suffering Prophet.

In Jeremiah and Lamentations, He is the Weeping Prophet.

In Ezekiel, He is the wonderful Four-Faced Man.

In Daniel, He is the Fourth Man in the midst of the fiery furnace.

In Hosea, He is my Love that is forever faithful.

In Joel, He is the Baptizer of the Holy Spirit.

In Amos, He is our burden Bearer.

In Obadiah, He is our Savior.

In Jonah, He is the great Foreign Missionary that takes the word of God into all the world.

In Micah, He is the Messenger with beautiful feet.

In Nahum, He is the avenger.

In Habakkuk, He is the Watchman that is ever praying for revival.

In Zephaniah, He is the Lord Mighty to serve.

In Haggai, He is the Restorer of our lost heritage.

In Zechariah, He is our Fountain.

In Malachi, He is the Son of Righteousness with healing in His wings.

In Matthew, He is the Christ, the Son of the Living God.

In Mark, He is the Miracle Worker.

In Luke, He is the Son of Man.

In John, He is the Door by which every one of us must enter.

In Acts, He is the Shining Light that appears to Saul on the road to
Damascus.

In Romans, He is our Justifier.

In 1 Corinthians, He is our Resurrection.

In 2 Corinthians, He is our Sin Bearer.

In Romans, He is our Justifier.

In Galatians, He redeems us from the law.

In Ephesians, He is our unsearchable Riches.

In 1 and 2 Thessalonians, He is our soon Coming King.

In Philippians, He supplies our every need.

In Colossians, He is the Fullness of the Godhead bodily.

In 1 and 2 Timothy, He is the Mediator between God and man.

In Titus, He is our Blessed Hope.

In Philemon, He is a Friend that sticks closer than a brother.

In Hebrews, He is the Blood of the Everlasting Covenant.

In James, He is the Lord that heals the sick.

In 1 and 2 Peter, He is our Chief Shepherd.

In 1, 2 and 3 John, it is Jesus who has the tenderness of Love.

In Jude, He is the Lord coming with 10,000 saints.

In Revelation, HE IS THE KING OF KINGS AND THE LORD OF LORDS!

— Camp Kirkland and Tom Fettke[3]

REVIEW QUESTIONS

1. What characterizes the beginning of the worship thread in Scripture?

2. Name ten different ways in which worship is expressed in the worship
    thread.

3. Describe the future of worship as it is foreshadowed in Revelation.

APPLICATION QUESTIONS

1. Each expression of worship in the worship thread is both response to the holiness of God *and* an act that keeps hearts and minds focused on God's holiness. Choose three expressions. How are they a response and how do they provide focus?

2. When are you most aware of the holiness of God? How do you respond to this holiness?

3. Worship as a lifestyle characterizes much of the worship thread. What are five characteristics of worship as a lifestyle?

4. What are three ways that worship is integrated into your own lifestyle? How do these things make you more aware of God's holiness?

5. What is the danger of "worthless worship"?

6. What are the signs of "worthless worship"? How can we guard against it?

Endnotes

Scripture quotations are from the *New King James Version*.

1. Ralph P. Martin, *Worship in the Early Church* (Grand Rapids: Wm. B. Eerdmans Publishing Co, 1975), 39.
2. Jack Hayford, *The Reward of Worship: The Joy of Fellowship with a Personal God* (Grand Rapids: Chosen Books, 2007), 35.
3. "Name Above All Names" by Camp Kirkland and Tom Fettke. Copyright © 1993 Integrity's Hosanna! Music (ASCAP) (adm. at CapitolCMGPublishing.com) All rights reserved. Used by permission.

CHAPTER 4

WORSHIP IN UNLIKELY PLACES

Observing biblical characters who turned to worship as a natural response to extenuating circumstances can clue us in regarding worship's deeper meaning.

As a result of this lesson, you will be able to

- describe the relationship between Job's loss and his response to loss;
- describe the relationship between Abraham's obedience and his response to impending loss;
- describe the relationship between David's loss and his response;
- describe the relationship between Jehoshaphat's situation of approaching war and his response;
- describe the relationship between *worship* and *praise*.

Worship is like a deep, deep mine, filled with rare treasures waiting to be explored by seeking hearts.[1]

If worship is what it is, as defined by the way in which biblical characters like Job and Abraham used that word, it is not an exaggeration to say that most Christians have never truly worshipped.

"Worship is the one thing that affects everything."[2]

One thing I ask from the Lord, this only do I seek: that I may dwell in the house of the Lord all the days of my life, to gaze on the beauty of the Lord and to seek him in His temple. For in the day of trouble he will keep me safe in his dwelling; he will hide me in the shelter of his sacred tent and set me high upon a rock (Psalm 27:4, 5, NIV).

Job: At this, Job got up and tore his robe and shaved his head. Then he fell to the ground in worship and said, "Naked I came from my mother's womb, and naked I will depart. The Lord gave and the Lord has taken away; may the name of the Lord be praised (Job 1:20, 21, NIV).

Abraham: And Abraham said to his young men, "Stay here with the donkey; the lad and I will go yonder and worship, and we will come back to you" (Genesis 22:5).

David: Then David got up from the ground. After he had washed, put on lotions and changed his clothes, he went into the house of the Lord and worshiped (2 Samuel 12:20, 21 NIV).

Jehoshaphat: And when he had consulted with the people, he appointed those who should sing to the Lord, and who should praise the beauty of holiness, as they went out before the army and were saying: "Praise the Lord, For His mercy endures forever' Now when they began to sing and to praise, the Lord set ambushes against the people of Ammon, Moab, and Mount Seir, who had come against Judah; and they were defeated (2 Chronicles 20:21, 22).

W e grow in our understanding of worship by observing the ways in which the word *worship* is used throughout the Scriptures—the root words used for worship, the context, emerging patterns, etc.

One of the patterns we can observe is the unlikely places or contexts in which the word *worship* is used, situations in which the term *worship* would not likely cross our minds. This lesson is devoted to looking at some of those occurrences, beginning with the familiar story of Job.

JOB

He is described in Scripture as "blameless and upright" (above reproach), a man who feared God and hated evil. He had ten children (seven sons and three daughters), and possessed great wealth. Among the men of the East, none had greater influence, none was more exemplary, than the man, Job (Job 1:1–3).

But Job's story suddenly takes a tragic turn. In a meeting in the spiritual realm in which "the sons of God presented themselves before the Lord," Satan was given permission to test Job. So, one by one, Job's servants came bearing bad news about the loss of his vast livestock, the destruction of his property, and finally, the deaths of his children. What is believed to be a tornado swept across Job's farm, taking the lives of his ten children all at once. Psychologists agree that the loss of a child is the most painful experience a parent can endure. That pain is multiplied when a parent loses more than one child, but losing ten children on the same day makes Job's experience very unique. That's why his reaction to the news is so remarkable:

> Then Job arose, tore his robe, and shaved his head; and he fell to the ground and worshiped. And he said:

> "Naked I came from my mother's womb,
> And naked shall I return there.
> The Lord gave, and the Lord has taken away;
> Blessed be the name of the Lord" (Job 1:20, 21).

It is believed that Job is the author of the book of Job. His use of the word *worship* in his reaction is therefore of special note. How likely is it that you would honestly describe your reaction to such personal loss as worship?

ABRAHAM

We continue by looking at another familiar account, this time in the life of Abraham. One can only imagine the burden he must have felt when instructed by God to offer his son Isaac as a sacrifice. His walk with God revolved around God's promise to give him a son through which he would become the father of a great nation. The logical question is how in the world is that going to happen if he offers up the young boy as a sacrifice? Yet, "by faith, Abraham obeyed" (Hebrews 11:8). The account of the story in Genesis 22 suggests that Abraham didn't sleep very well that night. He arose early in the morning, split the wood and saddled the donkey himself (tasks usually reserved for servants), and set out on the long journey to the place to which God had instructed him to go (vv. 3, 4). This wasn't a quick drive across town; no quick visit to the pediatrician's office. It was a three-day journey—by foot, across rugged terrain. There was time for Abraham to contemplate what he was about to do, to grieve the pending loss of the child who had come to mean so much to him, to symbolize the covenant God had made with him. And yet we're told that when Abraham lifted his eyes and saw the place of the sacrifice (Mount Moriah), he offered this word of instruction to his servants: "Stay here with the donkey; the lad and I will go yonder and worship, and we will come back to you" (v. 5).

Once again, please notice the use of the word *worship* in Abraham's instructions to his servants. Is it likely that the word *worship* would even be part of your thought process, knowing that you are about to offer up your only son as a sacrifice?

DAVID

We turn next to the familiar story of 2 Samuel 12 in which the prophet Nathan confronts David about his sin. David's trespass is doubled because he not only committed adultery with Bathsheba, he arranged for the death of her husband. Considering that David was a man after God's own heart—a person who was very sensitive to the possibility of grieving the Holy Spirit, to hurting God's heart—it's likely that the burden of this experience weighed more heavily on him than any difficulty he had ever endured.

In addition to the Prophet's rebuke and broken fellowship with God, David suffered the devastating consequences of the death of the child conceived through his adulterous affair (vv. 12–14). So heavy was the pain that David mourned and did not eat for seven days. But everything changed when the child died: "Then David got up from the ground. After he had washed, put on lotions and changed his clothes, he went into the house of the Lord and worshiped" (NIV).

It was noted earlier that the loss of a child is the most painful experience a parent can endure. Yet, David's response to this very personal and painful experience was worship. Marred by the failure and guilt of adultery and murder, compounded by the pain of the loss of a child, David went into the house of the Lord and set his gaze upon Him in worship.

Why this response? How likely is it that you would worship if caught in the vortex of such misery?

The answer is found in this testimony from David's own pen: "One thing I ask from the Lord, this only do I seek: that I may dwell in the house of the Lord all the days of my life, to gaze on the beauty of the Lord and to seek Him in His temple. For in the day of trouble He will keep me safe in his dwelling; He will hide me in the shelter of his sacred tent and set me high upon a rock" (Psalm 27:4, 5, NIV). The sweet singer of Israel, the man after God's own heart, Israel's shepherd king, narrowed all of life's desires down to one. Not protection in battle, nor revenge on his enemies, nor the prosperity of his kingdom, but the blessings of forever gazing on the beauty of the Lord in His house. This is worship, the one thing that affects everything. It is David's chief desire, so he turned to it even in his darkest hour.

JEHOSHAPHAT

Finally, we turn to a story in 2 Chronicles 20 for one more example of worship in an unlikely situation. Judah's King Jehoshaphat had just gotten word that a vast army was approaching. In twenty-first century terms, this would be the equivalent of the armies of Jordan, Iran, and Syria combining their military strengths to fight against Israel. So in desperation, Jehoshaphat proclaimed a fast and sought the Lord. The final line of his prayer is deeply moving: "For we have no power against this great multitude that is coming against us; nor do we know what to do, but our eyes are upon You" (20:12). So with eyes on the Lord and assurance of His presence and victory, they executed an amazing war strategy: A choir was formed to lead the way into battle! We read in verse 21, "And when he had consulted with the people, he appointed those who should sing to the Lord, and who should praise the beauty of holiness, as they went out before the army and were saying: 'Praise the Lord, for His mercy endures forever.'"

It turned out that as Judah worshipped the Lord in the midst of the battle, the invading armies were supernaturally ambushed and turned on each other. At the end of the day God's people prevailed, not by the sword, but through the power of worship.

It is noteworthy that the word used in this account is *praise*, not *worship*, and there is general agreement that these two words aren't synonymous. Worship may involve our audible praise, but as we've observed in these biblical accounts, worship is so much more. And yet we shouldn't forget that God desires the praise of His people—"the fruit of our lips" (see Hebrews 13:15)—and that there is tremendous power in praise when it is used to exalt the greatness and majesty of our God. Praise is a natural response of the worshipping heart, which is why these words are often used interchangeably.

Here again, we are invited to consider whether or not worship would have been part of our thinking if faced with that situation. Facing a showdown with a vast army, would you think to form a choir or worship team to lead the way into battle?

THE ULTIMATE QUESTION

The ultimate question is this: What do the stories of Job's tragedy, Abraham's ultimate test, David's response to the death of his child, and Jehoshaphat's experience in battle teach us about worship?

These accounts teach us that these men of old had a view of worship that was vastly different from that of most contemporary Christians. For Job, it was the affirmation of God's sovereign rule and providence in all things. For Abraham, it was submission to the will of God, the willingness to offer up that which meant the most to him, placing full confidence and trust in the God who provides. For David, it was acknowledgment of sin and the rightness of God's justice (in the taking the life of the child), confronting carnality and pride, and submission to worship's purifying and restorative power. And for Jehoshaphat, worship was a weapon of warfare, the key to spiritual victory and the establishment of God's rule in the earth. "For Thine is the kingdom, the power, and the glory, forever and ever, amen." This closing line from Jesus' model prayer about His sovereign rule in the earth is ultimately about worship, a reminder that these references to worship explored in this chapter are only "unlikely" because of how far we've strayed from worship's core meaning. For Job, Abraham, and David, there was no glamor and glitz of sound and stage lights, no worship band and favorite choruses, just heart and soul turned toward God—and as for Jehoshaphat, the choir he started was all about the splendor of God's holiness. Not that the elements of contemporary worship here mentioned are wrong, but focusing on our satisfaction instead of God's glory can cause worship to be drained of its substance and become idolatry. So may these thoughts move us to repent of "the things we've made it," moving us back to the heart of worship.

REVIEW QUESTIONS

1. What is the relationship between Job's loss and his response to it? Why did he respond the way he did?

2. What is the relationship between Abraham's obedience and his response to impending loss?

3. What is the relationship between David's loss and his response?

4. What is the relationship between Jehoshaphat's situation of approaching war and his response?

5. What is the difference between *worship* and *praise*? How are the two words related to one another?

APPLICATION QUESTIONS

1. What do you mean when you say that you *respect* someone? When you want to communicate to that individual that you respect them, what characterizes your behavior toward them?

2. The Hebrew word used to indicate both Job's and Abraham's worship paints a picture of bowing down out of respect for a superior. In other words, their worship of God included a manifestation of an attitude of respect. What are three ways in which your own worship can manifest an attitude of respect for God?

3. When we value something, we tend to want to protect it at all costs. This is true for our personal preferences, our possessions, and our customs. What are five things that you value?

4. The English etymology of the word *worship* is *worth-ship*. In one layer of their worship, Job and Abraham were bowing down before the Lord to tell Him that He was *worth more* than what they had lost, or the loss they were facing. How can you communicate to God that He is worth more than each of those five things that you highly value, even when you aren't facing tragedy?

5. Recall the relationship between the words *worship* and *praise*. Is it possible to "praise" God without truly worshipping Him? How can you avoid being guilty of this?

Endnotes

Scripture quotations are from the *New King James Version*, unless otherwise noted.

1. Adapted from "Thy Word is Like a Garden, Lord," Edwin Hodder.
2. Scott Brown in message delivered during The Worship of God conference, Ridgecrest, NC, 2013.

CHAPTER 5

PARSING WORSHIP WORDS

Examining those words for *worship* found in the Bible's original languages and considering their commonly held definitions will enhance our worship quotient and even the quality of our worship.

After reading this chapter, you will be able to

- list and define five words that contribute to our understanding of the word *worship*;
- define *transactional worship*;
- list five characteristics of God-honoring worship.

Worship is the submission of all our nature to God. It is the quickening of the

conscience by his holiness; the nourishment of mind with his truth; the purifying of imagination by his beauty; the opening of the heart to his love; the surrender of will to his purpose—all this gathered up in adoration, the most selfless emotion of which our nature is capable.[1]

Therefore, I urge you, brothers and sisters, in view of God's mercy, to offer your bodies as a living sacrifice, holy and pleasing to God—this is your true and proper worship. Do not conform to the pattern of this world, but be transformed by the renewing of your mind. Then you will be able to test and approve what God's will is—his good, pleasing and perfect will (Romans 12:1, 2, NIV).

———————————

A ll of human history will someday narrow down to one thing: the ceaseless worship of the Lamb of glory upon His throne. For that reason, the most important question Christians can ask is: How then, shall we worship?

Answering that question should begin with a working definition of worship. How can we know how to worship if we don't know what worship means in the first place? The challenge, though, is that while much is said in Scripture about worship, nothing is offered in terms of a "dictionary type" definition. In other words, there's no "worship is…" verse in the Bible. Nonetheless, drawing upon the many things Scripture does say about it and the words used for worship in the Bible's original languages, we can better understand the meaning of this very important word.

The following paragraphs are therefore given to "parsing"—examining, analyzing, observing—those words in the original languages from which our English word *worship* is translated.

But before we look at other languages, let's take note of the root word in English. The word *worship* is rooted in the old English word *worth-ship*, which denotes ascribing worth or value to something or someone. We speak of gold and other precious metals in terms of their value. Because of its worth, we would be completely awed if a Stradivarius violin were placed in our hands. We honor monarchs in recognition of their majesty and authority. And similarly, in an even greater way, we are to hold God in highest honor, esteem, reverence, and awe because of His inestimable worth and intrinsic value. Ascribing such worth to God is the focus of the old English word from which the word *worship* is derived.

HEBREW WORDS

Moving on to the Scriptures, we find two words for *worship* in the Old Testament: *shachah*, meaning to bow down, to prostrate oneself, and *abad*, to serve, to offer sacrifice, to give an offering.

The combined meaning of these two Hebrew words is showing reverence and awe, giving honor and devotion, demonstrated in tangible action—offering a sacrifice.

GREEK WORDS

We also find two words in the New Testament: *proskuneo*, meaning to kiss, show affection, and *latreuo*, meaning to serve, offer sacrifice.

The combined meaning of these two Greek words is to tangibly demonstrate love and affection, rendering heartfelt devotion and service.

COMBINING HEBREW AND GREEK

As these Hebrew and Greek words illustrate, the meaning of the word *worship* correlates beautifully across the Testaments. The Hebrew *shachah* and Greek *proskuneo* correspond, having very similar meanings, and the Hebrew *abad* and Greek *lautreuo* also correspond, having the same meaning. This explains why, depending on the Bible version, "reasonable worship" and "reasonable service" are used interchangeably in the commonly quoted Romans 12:1. This isn't a mistranslation; it is because the Greek word for *worship* in that verse actually means service or to serve.

All together, these four words reflect the actions of someone expressing deep love and affection for another. Pastor Bob Coy provides a helpful illustration of this in a 2007 *Decision* magazine article, as follows:

> ...a man stands outside his girlfriend's window, singing a serenade for
> the whole world to hear. He doesn't have the slightest care what others
> think. He only knows that all the affection bubbling up in his heart

can no longer be contained. And as he unashamedly looks for the best expression of what he is feeling, he suddenly begins kissing his hands and throwing them toward the one he loves. It doesn't matter what anyone else thinks of him, because the one he loves is well worth the display of emotion.[2]

WORSHIP AT ITS CORE

The purpose of parsing these root words is to deepen our understanding of worship's core meaning. What is worship when all is swept away?

Skye Jethani (of Up from Ur) offers important insights on this topic. He is quoted in a Fall 2013 *Leadership Journal* article titled "What Denomination Gives the Most?" He cautions that trying to get to the heart of worship is where the problem of worship often begins, especially for Americans who place such high value on the pragmatic, the utilitarian, and the transactional. We care much about what works, what's most practical, and negotiating deals. In and of itself, this isn't a problem. But when we transfer this approach to our worship of God, the American version of the golden calf emerges! Its worshippers ask, "What new thing can we do to get to the next level?" They demand practical sermons—on being prosperous, having a better marriage, becoming a better version of their old self. So worship becomes transactional—we expect something in return for what we give to God.

As a prime example, Jethani cites this tweet directed at God by an NFL player after losing a game: "I praise you 24/7!!! And this is how you do me!!! You expect me to learn from this??? How??? I will never forget this!! Ever!!"[3]

This exposes the serious state of worship in our day. It's become a means to an end. Jethani's assertion is therefore timely: "...God does not exist to be useful. God exists to be adored, simply because of who he is. True worship is never transactional."[4]

At its core, true worship is giving God all that we are and have, no matter how costly, expecting nothing in return. This principle has scriptural backing, including the story of the woman who poured an entire alabaster jar of very costly perfume on Jesus in selfless worship (see Mark 14:2–4). Those looking on called it a waste; the woman considered it her reasonable sacrifice. Her extravagance reflected the depth of her love.

It is therefore reasonable to infer from this that most of us have never truly worshipped God—in "a seemingly wasteful extravagance" with one desire: "to behold the beauty of the Lord" (Psalm 27:4). This is worship's call; may our souls say "Yes!"

COMMON DEFINITIONS

Having looked at the root words for *worship* and what they teach us about its core meaning, we will conclude this chapter by meditating on some of its common definitions, crafted by spiritual leaders and worship practitioners who have delved deeply into Scripture to discover the core meaning of worship. Beginning with one of the most widely quoted definitions in circulation, crafted by William Temple, former archbishop of Canterbury (1821–1902), it moves beyond the trendy feel-good notions about worship that pervade the contemporary church to something much deeper, richer, fuller, and which encompasses the full gamut of our experience with God. Other definitions are included to reflect the basic understanding of worship as our response (individually and corporately) to God's revelation of Himself. Others reflect the fact that worship involves the whole person—the affection of the heart and attention of the mind, and we are finally reminded that worship is more than weekly church activity, that true worship is 24/7—a lifestyle. That is not to suggest that worship as a weekly activity isn't important. We are admonished in Scripture to not forsake the regular assembly of the saints (Hebrews 10:25). Rather, it is a reminder that we are to view everything we do as worship, and that God can receive as much glory through our mundane activities as from a corporate worship activity. That is Paul's passion in Romans 12:1: "I beseech you therefore, brethren, by the mercies of God, that you present your bodies a living sacrifice, holy, acceptable to God, which is your reasonable service." Worship is more than giving an offering; it is our becoming the offering. So let's read these definitions slowly, allowing them to sink deep into our hearts.

- Worship is the submission of our nature to God; the quickening of the conscience by His holiness; the nourishment of mind with His truth; the purifying of imagination by His beauty; the opening of the heart to His love; the surrender of our will to His purpose. All this, gathered up in adoration, is the most selfless emotion of which the human nature is capable.
- Worship is the believer's affirmative response to God's self-revelation,

the active response of a community of believers to the glory of God, attributing praise and honor for who He is, and for what He has done.

- Worship is the believer's heart response to God's character, attributes, and the truth of His Word.
- Worship is communion and intimacy with God, the act of joyously loving and celebrating God, the highest and most fulfilling activity in which believers can engage.
- Worship is focusing the mind's attention and the heart's affection on the love, grace, and mercy of God, which daily informs and guides our actions and experiences.
- Worship is a lifestyle.

IN SUMMARY

Defining *worship* isn't easy; it is a big and multifaceted subject. But we must work at it, because it is the one thing that affects everything. Based on the root words looked at in this chapter, worship is ascribing ultimate worth and value to God. It is holding God in highest esteem, reverence and awe, our lives being an expression of deepest affection and devotion. It is the giving of our all in sacrifice to Him who gave His all for our redemption. It's loving God purely and simply for who He is and for His mighty deeds. It isn't transactional. We shouldn't love God for what we'll get from Him in return. We worship Him because He is God alone and deserves our worship.

Worshipping God is therefore the most important activity in which Christians can engage. The true measurement of a church is its capacity to honor God with biblical worship. All of life and ministry should flow from our preoccupation with the worship of God. These truths should motivate a lifelong quest to explore the deeper meaning of worship and to experience it more fully.

REVIEW QUESTIONS

1. What are five words—and their definitions—that contribute to our understanding of the word *worship*?

2. What is *transactional worship?*

3. List five characteristics of God-honoring worship.

APPLICATION QUESTIONS

1. What is something in your life—besides faith or family—that is "worth something" to you? How do your actions declare its worth?

2. Compare and contrast how you show worth to temporal things with how God desires to be worshipped.

3. In what ways is your worship of God "transactional"?

4. Drawing on the definitions given in this chapter, how would you define *worship* in your own words?

Endnotes

Scripture quotations are from the *New King James Version* unless otherwise noted.

1. William Temple, https://www.goodreads.com/author/quotes/397351.William_Temple. Web accessed 9-3-15.
2. Bob Coy, "Is Your Worship Worthship?" *Decision*, February 27, 2007, http://billygraham.org/decision-magazine/march-2007/is-your-worship-worthship/. Web accessed 9-3-15.
3. Skye Jethani, *With: Reimagining the Way You Relate to God* (Nashville: Thomas Nelson, 2011), 27.
4. Jethani, *Leadership Journal*, Fall 2013, http://www.christianitytoday.com/le/2013/fall/accounting-for-generosity.html. Web access 9-3-15.

CHAPTER 6

A THEOLOGY
OF WORSHIP

In worship, God is recognized and honored for who He is, humans become what they were created to be, the beauty and worth of God is declared to the world, and God's will is done on earth as it is in heaven.

After reading this chapter, you will be able to

- describe the pattern of revelation, recognition, and response as it relates to worship, listing three examples of the revelation, recognition, and response pattern from Scripture;

- explain how worship recognizes and honors God for who He is;

- describe how worship causes humans to become what they were created to be;

- discuss how worship can effectively declare the beauty and worth of God to the world;

- compare and contrast earthly worship with heavenly worship;

- explain how worship is part of God's will being done on earth as it is in heaven.

Worthy are You, our Lord and our God, to receive glory and honor and power (Revelation 4:11).

All worship is driven by a theology, even if unconsciously.[1]

D o you remember Samuel's call in 1 Samuel 3? God called repeatedly, but Samuel didn't *respond* until it was *revealed* to him by Eli that God was calling and Samuel *recognized* God's voice.

What about Job's encounter with God? After the arguments between Job and his friends, God spoke, *revealing* Himself (Job 38–39, 41). *Recognizing* God for who He is, Job was able to *respond* appropriately (Job 40, 42).

And think of Isaiah, receiving his prophetic call in Isaiah 6. As God *revealed* Himself in His glory, Isaiah *recognized* God for who He is and *responded* in kind.

One final example is Thomas. After Thomas doubted Christ's resurrection, Jesus *revealed* Himself, Thomas *recognized* Him, and *responded*, "My Lord and my God!" (John 20:28).

What we see in each of these examples is the pattern of worship that can be observed throughout Scripture. Everything begins with God revealing Himself. Because of this *revelation*, people can *recognize* God for who He is. They can then *respond* to God in worship.

We experience this pattern of revelation, recognition, and response in our daily lives as well.

I have a friend with poor eyesight. However, I was not always aware of this because he disguises it well. One day he visited my church and was walking directly toward me. From about forty feet away I began indicating that I recognized him. He approached me with no sign of recognition, aloof and unaware of my presence. The distance closed to twenty feet and still nothing.

As he got within fifteen feet I got anxious, wondering if I had offended him or if he even recognized me. Finally, five feet away he saw me and responded. His eyes lit up, he looked directly at me and smiled. Later, I learned that with his limited vision, he truly had not seen me until I was close enough to shake his hand.

In order for my friend to recognize me I had to reveal myself to him by drawing closer.

Another memory comes to mind from when I was attending a private Christian boarding school. I had a crush on a classmate and our school traveled to visit her home church. The students were responsible for the service and I was preaching. I was very nervous about the prospect of meeting her family, particularly her father. From the moment I entered the building I was preoccupied with trying to identify him. During the course of the evening I went into the sound booth to get my microphone arranged. I visited with the sound man while I was there. I tried to be gracious, but all I could think about was how anxious I was to meet the girl's father. Later that night she introduced her family to me and I met her dad. Of course, it was my second time meeting him. He was the soundman! My mind swirled as I tried to recall what kind of first impression I must have made on him. I wondered if my response to him had been appropriate.

In order for me to respond appropriately, I needed him to be revealed to me in a way that I recognized who he was.

From these two stories, we gather a few key insights regarding the pattern of worship in Scripture:

Our response to God cannot exceed our level of recognition.

Our recognition of God cannot exceed His level of revelation.

Thus worship always begins with God's initiative in revealing Himself. Only then can we recognize Him and respond in faith. Thankfully, God has revealed Himself throughout history and chiefly in Jesus Christ. He has drawn near to us so that we can recognize Him and respond appropriately.

As we observe this pattern of worship in Scripture, four central elements of worship emerge to form a theology of worship. By theology of worship, I mean a biblical understanding of why we worship and what worship accomplishes. Let us consider these four major elements of a theology of worship.

ONE: In worship, God is recognized and honored for who He is.

In the most extended worship scene in Scripture (Revelation 4, 5) we see God revealed and recognized as Creator of everything. In response, the heavenly chorus sings,

> "Worthy are You, our Lord and our God, to receive glory and honor and power; for You created all things, and because of Your will they existed, and were created" (Revelation 4:11).

This passage reminds me of a story about a group of scientists who developed the technology to create a human from the raw materials found in the earth's soil. Proud of their accomplishment, they challenged God to a human-making contest. God agreed and the participants prepared to create their humans. But as they stooped down with bucket and spade to collect the soil for their experiment, God interrupted, "Sorry, first make your own dirt!"

This story reminds us that without God's creative work, nothing but God would exist (Genesis 1:1; John 1:1-3; Colossians 1:16, 17). In worship we recognize that we owe our very existence, and the existence of all other things, to God alone.

Back to Revelation 4-5 we also see that God is revealed and recognized as Redeemer. All of creation lifts its voice in unison to proclaim,

> "Worthy is the Lamb that was slain to receive power and riches and wisdom and might and honor and glory and blessing" (Revelation 5:12).

This passage calls to mind the story of a man who came across a burning home in his village. Hearing the screams of children inside, the man ran in and emerged, badly burned, but with a child under each arm. The parents of the children perished in the fire and the children were put up for adoption. A wealthy individual in the village wanted to appear generous, so he offered to adopt the children and give them every luxury he could afford. Just as the judge was going to award custody, the man who had saved them from the fire made his plea to adopt them. The judge asked on what grounds the man believed that he would be a more suitable father than his wealthy competitor. The man made no verbal response, but simply lifted up his hands to show the scars from his burns. He was awarded custody of the children.[2] It is because of Christ's work on the cross that we belong to Him. His sacrifice was the price of our redemption, His death the ransom for our lives.

Worship is fundamentally about recognizing God as the one who has both Created and Redeemed us.

What effect should this recognition have on our response to God?

Our worship gatherings should always take advantage of the opportunity to enact the gospel in both forms and signs. If worship is about recognizing and responding to God as Creator and Redeemer, then this should be obvious in every aspect of our corporate worship: the words we sing, the attitude of our hearts, the symbols we incorporate, the layout and décor of the worship space, the posture of our bodies, etc.

As the late Robert Webber notes, worship is an enactment of what he calls "the drama of redemption." God became incarnate in Christ to commune with us and we commune with Him as embodied creatures. Thus, worship is incarnate, it is played out in outward, physical activities. These activities are no mere signs or rituals, but outward demonstrations of an inward reality. They symbolize our relationship with God.[3]

In daily life, we must commit ourselves to responding appropriately to our recognition of God's revelation as all in all. As God reveals Himself as

Creator, we respond as creatures, submitting to Him for our design and purpose.

Beautiful, we respond in adoration of His glory.

Powerful, we respond in fear and awe of His majesty.

King, we respond in humble service as His servants.

Our Savior, we respond in faith to His salvation and sanctifying work.

The Savior of the world, we respond in obedience to the Great Commission.

We worship God for who God is and what God does. We only know the former by the latter. But as God reveals His character through His works, we recognize and respond to Him. This is worship.

TWO: In worship, humans become what they were created to be.

Humans were created in the image of God (Gen 1:26–27). The introduction of sin and death marred and obscured this image. But in relationship with God, we are transformed into the image of Christ, as He redeems and restores what was lost in the Fall. As a result, humans become what they were created to be: image-bearing worshipers of God.

In his book *We Become What We Worship*, Greg Beale argues for this simple thesis:

> "What people revere, they resemble, either for ruin or for restoration."[4]

If it is true that we become what we worship—and Scripture seems to support this assertion—then one of the greatest challenges we face is asking, "What am I becoming?"

Not only must we ask this, but we must be honest enough to identify the answer to this question as the true object of our worship.

So, what are you becoming?

Paul faced the Romans with the same question when he wrote,

> Do not be conformed to this world, but be transformed by the renewing of your mind, so that you may prove what the will of God is, that which is good and acceptable and perfect (Romans 12:2).

Paul offers two options. You can either be forced into the mold of the world around you, a mold of sin and death, or you can be transformed into the very image of God. So ask yourself, *Am I being conformed to the world? Do I look more and more like the world each day?*

If the answer is yes, then you are worshipping the world. Remember, you become what you worship.

On the other hand, you can ask, *Am I being transformed into the image of Christ? Do I progressively look more like Jesus?*

If the answer is yes, then you are worshipping God. As Jack Hayford has said, "Worship changes the worshiper into the image of the One worshiped."

Of course, if your view of worship is limited to singing a few songs during church, then this will seem like an overwhelming burden. How can we worship every moment of our life, when we have so many things pulling on our attention at work and home and school? Here is where we must broaden our vision of worship to understand that every activity of our life is supposed to be offered in worship to God. As Paul wrote to the Corinthians, "Whether, then, you eat or drink or whatever you do, do all to the glory of God" (1 Corinthians 10:31).

You were created to be a worshipper of God, in every aspect of your life. God created you for rest, responsibility, and relationships, each of which can bring honor and glory to God when they are devoted to Him.

In 1979 the Grammy for Best Rock Vocal Performance by a Male was given to Bob Dylan for his song "Gotta Serve Somebody." The chorus reminds us that whether we're serving the Devil or serving the Lord, we've got to serve somebody.

In response, John Lennon penned the song "Serve Yourself." But Dylan understood something that Lennon did not. Something Martin Luther wrote at length about in *The Bondage of the Will*, where he compared our human will to a donkey that must be directed by a rider. We will either be driven by sin and death or we will be driven by Christ and righteousness.[5] We never belong to ourselves, but always to a Master. The Master we serve is the one we are worshipping.

One of my favorite songs is "When I Look Into Your Holiness," by Wayne and Cathy Perrin. In this song they remind us that the reason we live is to worship God.

May we ever live to worship Him.

As we worship God we gaze upon His glorious face and this gazing results in our transformation into the image of Christ. We read about this incredible process in 2 Corinthians 3:18:

But we all, with unveiled face, beholding as in a mirror the glory of the Lord, are being transformed into the same image from glory to glory, just as from the Lord, the Spirit.

This ongoing process of transformation is taking place even while we're beholding Jesus through a dark glass, knowing and seeing only in part (1 Corinthians 13:9–12). However, the time will come when Christ will return and we will see Him in all His glory. In that moment we will be completely transformed into His image,

> Beloved, now we are children of God, and it has not appeared as yet
> what we will be. We know that when He appears, we will be like Him,
> because we will see Him just as He is (1 John 3:2).

We become what we worship. So let us worship Jesus Christ and watch as we are transformed into His image, becoming what we were created to be.

THREE: In worship, the beauty and worth of God is declared to the world.

One of the recent movements in Christianity is to recognize that worship should serve, not only to build up the church, but also as a form of evangelism.[6] While this might be a recent emphasis of the church in North America, it is by no means a new idea. Consider the message of Psalm 96 in which the people of God are instructed to worship the majesty and worth of God in such a way that the world sees them and responds in kind.

Worship is not simply a private act of the church, it is intended to be a public declaration of God's worth so that the world can see Him for who He is.

God has not only revealed Himself through creation, Scripture, and Christ, but He continues to reveal Himself by His Holy Spirit through the church.

We see this phenomenon in Acts 2, a situation in which public worship became an opportunity for evangelistic outreach. As the people of God worshipped, the world was drawn to the experience and received the gospel message. Three thousand people were saved because 120 people were willing to worship God.

While our worship services should be designed for the living, they must also serve as an invitation to the dead. We should take care not to make our corporate worship inaccessible. While it must be Christ-centric, it need not be Christian-centric. In other words, it is not intended to fulfill our personal preferences, but to glorify God, edify the church, and invite the world to join us.

Pastor John Piper's well-known saying that "Missions exist because worship doesn't" was mentioned earlier. Reflect on that again for a moment. We are on a mission to take the gospel to the world because there are still people who do not worship God. Once everyone has bowed the knee and confessed that Jesus Christ is Lord to the glory of God the Father, there will be no need for missions. But worship will go on for eternity. In Piper's final sermon to Bethlehem Baptist Church, he said,

Seeking the worship of the nations is fueled by the joy of our own worship. You can't commend what you don't cherish. You can't proclaim what you don't prize.

Worship is the fuel and the goal of missions.[7]

Jesus speaks of worship as evangelism in Matthew 5:14–16. As we openly serve and worship God, our light shines to those around us and they are invited to glorify God. For this reason, Jesus calls us as a city on a hill, a shining beacon to the world. Let us be a beacon that clearly points the way to God and invites unbelievers to join us in worship.

FOUR: In worship, God's will is done on earth as it is in heaven.

There is an old saying, "Pray like everything depends upon God, work like everything depends upon you." Jesus instructed us to pray,

"Your kingdom come,
Your will be done,
On earth as it is in heaven" (Matthew 6:10).

When we worship, we are putting this prayer into action. The kingdom comes to earth when we worship because worship is the fundamental activity of the kingdom. Sadly, this has been misrepresented in artistic and popular visions of "heaven" in which everyone is given a harp and expected to sit on a cloud playing music for all eternity. But this limited view of worship is not what we mean by saying worship is the fundamental activity of the kingdom. Rather, we are thinking of worship broadly in terms of loving service and devotion to God. This will be our joy for all eternity and we are invited to begin that eternal life of worship here and now. When we do, the kingdom of God comes to earth.

As the kingdom comes, the earth and its people are prepared for the eternal kingdom that is to come. This recognition helps us to more fully appreciate the repeated references to worship throughout Scripture, particularly the book of Revelation. The purpose of Revelation is not so that we could *predict* and *propagandize* in time, but so that we can *prepare* for eternity. Revelation opens our eyes to the heavens, not so that we can escape from earth, but so that we can be an active participant in heaven coming to earth. That is why Revelation is fundamentally a book about worship.

So worship God. Not only is it good practice for eternity, but it brings eternity into time. It ushers the kingdom of God into the earth.

CONCLUSION

So, let's look back and summarize our four-point theology of worship. First, in worship, God is recognized and honored for who He is. Second, in worship, humans become what they were created to be. Third, in worship, the beauty and worth of God is declared to the world. Finally, in worship, God's will is done on earth as it is in heaven. May our worship, both individually and corporately, be marked by an increasing awareness of what worship is and does.

REVIEW QUESTIONS

1. Describe the revelation–recognition–response pattern in scripture. List three examples.

2. How does worship recognize and honor God for who He is?

3. How does worship cause humans to become what they were created to be?

4. How can worship effectively declare the beauty and worth of God to the world?

5. Compare and contrast earthly worship with heavenly worship.

6. How is worship part of God's will being done on earth as it is in heaven?

APPLICATION QUESTIONS

1. Who do you recognize God to be?

2. Choose five of the attributes you listed above. How are you responding to each of these? Is your response appropriate?

3. How are you seeing the image of God being restored in you as you worship?

4. How is your worship—both individually and corporately—declaring God's beauty and worship to the world? Is your worship causing people of the world to glorify God?

5. How are you actively praying for and anticipating that the kingdom of God is filling the earth? How is your worship—individually and corporately—making the kingdom of God visible/tangible on earth?

Endnotes

Scripture quotations in this chapter are from the *New American Standard Bible*.

1. Covenant Fellowship Lake Dallas, *A Theology of Worship* (http://www.cfld.org/theology-of-worship.html). Web accessed 4-16-15.
2. This story is adapted from Graham H. Twelftree, *Your Point Being?* (London: Monarch Books, 2003), 169.
3. Robert E. Webber, *Worship: Old & New, Revised Edition* (Grand Rapids: Zondervan, 1994), 85.
4. Quote taken from Tony Reinke, "We Become What We Worship," online blog post (http://www.desiring-god.org/articles/we-become-what-we-worship). Web accessed 3-19-15.
5. Martin Luther, *The Bondage of the Will*, translated by J. I. Packer and O. R. Johnston (Grand Rapids: Baker Books, 2002).
6. See, for example, Sally Morgenthaler, *Worship Evangelism* (Grand Rapids: Zondervan, 1995).
7. http://www.desiringgod.org/sermons/missions-exists-because-worship-doesnt-a-bethlehem-legacy-inherited-and-bequeathed. Web accessed 3-26-15.

CHAPTER 7

WORSHIP LESSONS FROM CHRISTIAN HISTORY

By studying the history of Christian worship, we can receive instruction and admonition as we seek to worship God more faithfully today and in the future.

After reading this chapter, you will be able to

- identify three insights supporting the significance of studying history as it relates to developing a theology and practice of worship;
- list the three major eras of Christian history;
- list five features that characterize worship in each of the major eras of Christian history.

I write so that you will know how one ought to conduct himself in the household of God, which is the church of the living God, the pillar and support of the truth (1 Timothy 3:15).

God cares about history.

He is God, not only of biblical history, but the history of the Christian church since the time of Scripture.

We [authors Whaid Rose and Israel Steinmetz] are leaders within the General Conference of the Church of God (Seventh Day). The history, identity and practice of our denomination has been influenced in significant ways by the Pietist, Baptist and Holiness traditions. Like many evangelical groups that share these influences, our style of worship today has been heavily influenced by the Free Church tradition and the impact of the Charismatic renewal movement.

In this chapter we'll make specific reference to how our particular denomination's worship style and practices have been influenced by various eras of Christian history. While our story may differ from yours, we trust that this endeavor will be meaningful for you. As you read about the eras of Christian history and reflect on your own worship traditions, we invite you to engage in the same self-evaluation. Our stories may be different, but the lessons to be learned from them are often the same.

WHY DO WE WORSHIP THE WAY WE DO?

Have you ever wondered why we sit in rows while we listen to a sermon? Ever wonder why some expect the sermon to be twenty minutes, while others expect forty-five, sixty or ninety? Or why we stand when we sing or pray?

Ever wonder why we celebrate the Lord's Supper at a given frequency, while other Christians do so at different times? And what about the style of music we play and sing, or our posture in prayer? Why do we arrange our services the way we do, with singing preceding and following preaching?

Why is the front of a church called an altar, and why do we call people to it for prayer at the end of a service?

Despite the fact that we don't have a formal, written liturgy, we arrive every week with a fairly detailed and specific expectation of what is going to happen at our respective worship services. Those of us who meet regularly with the same group of Christians have a shared expectation with everyone else of what we will do, in what order, in which posture, and for how long. But where did all this come from?

Many assume that everything they do is taken directly from Scripture. They believe these activities, the order in which they're done, and the posture of the body and heart while doing them, are sacred. They assume that somewhere in the Bible we're told specifics regarding the shape that worship services are supposed to take.

But the reality is that Scripture provides very little in the way of direct instruction for structuring a worship service or even what should be included in the service. There is no specific liturgy given in the Bible, no approved list of instruments, no directions regarding seating arrangements, décor, or lighting. Nowhere can we find a clear answer as to whether we should sit, stand or kneel during any given activity of corporate worship. There's no indication of whether we should gather in rows facing forward or in circles facing each other. Such instructions just aren't there.

So, why do we do what we do? To borrow a line from *Fiddler on the Roof*, "Tradition!"

Now, saying that most of what we do in corporate worship services is inherited from past generations does not immediately tell us whether it's good or bad. It just means that our experience of corporate worship did not form in a vacuum. Rather, it has been shaped throughout history by Christians in other eras. We do what we do in large part because they did what they did. And our children and those we lead to the Lord will learn to worship from us, and the tradition will continue.

Some chafe at this idea and respond by insisting that we go "back to the Bible" to get our instructions. But as we noted before, Scripture gives very little in the way of specifics. The clarion call to worship in "spirit and truth" (John 4:23, 24), is not accompanied by concrete details. Rather, we must evaluate our traditions in the light of what Scripture does say about the true nature and object of worship. We must make choices about specific activities and sequences in our worship services based upon those broader principles. As part of that process, we must have at least a basic grasp of how our worship practices evolved through history and why they were created in the first place.

In his book *Worship: Old & New*, the late Robert Webber provides a concise overview of the history of Christian worship in three eras: Ancient and Medieval, Reformation and Free Church, and Twentieth Century Renewal Movements.[1] He begins his discussion of history by noting that while some are hesitant to study it, there is great value in understanding our past.[2]

From Webber we draw at least three insights for why we should study the history of worship. First, history matters to God. Not just biblical history, but the ongoing history of all God's people. If it matters to God, it should matter to us. Second, history provides context and background for our own faith and practice. As we've noted, Scripture is not the only source we rely on for creating our worship services. Knowing where our ideas and practices come from is important. Third, history provides both resources and warnings. By knowing the experience of those who came before us in worship we can receive insight and instruction from their positive, and negative, examples.

So, let us consider New Testament worship, and survey Webber's three eras of the history of Christian worship. Bear in mind that this brief survey looks specifically at the history of corporate worship gatherings, not the entire scope of what is meant by "worship." Also, this survey is limited to those developments in worship that most directly affect the worship practices of the Church of God (Seventh Day). Thus, this survey is an invitation to continued study of both history and Scripture.

NEW TESTAMENT WORSHIP (AD 35–100)

In the New Testament era, worship centered on the Word (i.e. Scripture) and the Table (i.e. communion) as an active, communal response to God's salvation in Christ. The Old Testament Scriptures were read and expounded upon as preachers and teachers explained how Jesus fulfilled them. As NT writings were disseminated, churches read them in their gatherings, drawing wisdom and instruction from the apostles. Many Bible scholars agree that at this point in history, Christians shared a common meal at most—if not all—of their corporate gatherings and that this meal included bread and wine, taken in remembrance of Christ's sacrifice and commemoration of the new covenant.

Beyond this reading of Scripture and common meal, the early worship gatherings were informal and varied from assembly to assembly. In many cases, they likely included elements of the synagogue model such as public reading of Scripture, singing and prayer. Paul's description of the meetings in Corinth indicate that they incorporated contributions from various members including psalms, teachings, revelations (i.e. knowledge, wisdom, prophecy), speaking in tongues, and interpretation (1 Corinthians 14:26).

Many of these primitive elements remain in our worship today, although changes can be observed, such as our frequency of taking communion and our limited inclusion of various gifts of the Spirit in our meetings.

ANCIENT WORSHIP (AD 100-400)

As the church spread throughout the Roman Empire, their meetings maintained a dual emphasis on the Word and the Table. However, they gradually became more regimented and uniform under the leadership of bishops and deacons. Webber's research reveals that they were likely broken into two services or liturgies (i.e. orders of service). One of these was open to the public and centered on the Word and one restricted for those who had been baptized and centered on the Table.

The first service included readings, singing, a sermon and reading the list of baptismal candidates. Then, those who were not yet baptized were dismissed and the baptized greeted one another with a kiss and received an offering. Communion was served—interspersed with readings of Scripture and singing. A thanksgiving was offered, followed by closing instructions and prayer.

These basic liturgies have formed the foundation for the order of service used in most of our meetings. We combine these elements of greeting, prayer, singing, collecting an offering and listening to a sermon in various ways, but we seldom meet without making space for each of them. When we do gather for our Lord's Supper Service we tend to include most of the elements included in Ancient Worship.

In addition to the regimentation of worship services during this time, there were also added certain ceremonial elements: a *Salutation* ("greeting"), the *Sursum Corda* ("Lift up your hearts") and the *Sanctus* ("Holy").

SALUTATION

Minister: "The Lord be with you", or "Peace be with you", or "The grace of the Lord Jesus Christ, the love of God and the communion of the Holy Ghost be with you all."

People: "And with thy spirit."

SURSUM CORDA

Minister: "Lift up your hearts!"

People: "We lift them up to the Lord!"

Minister: "Let us give thanks to the Lord!"

People: "It is meet and right to do so!"

SANCTUS

"Holy, Holy, Holy, Lord God Almighty, Heaven and earth are full of thy glory; glory be to thee; O Lord."

We can observe vestiges of these practices in our modern services, particularly in our Spanish-speaking congregations where it is common to hear the following interchange:

Minister: "Pas avos otros!" (Peace be unto you!)

People: "Avos pas!" (And unto you, peace!)

Beginning in the fourth century with the legalization—and later, official status—of Christianity, Christian worship became increasingly influenced by local culture. This local influence accounts for the emergence of major differences in Eastern and Western worship styles.

The Eastern churches were increasingly influenced by the Hellenistic emphasis on the arts and the aesthetic. As a result, Eastern churches began emphasizing beauty, art and decadent rituals. Conversely, the Western churches were influenced by the Roman emphasis on pragmatism. Accordingly, Western churches opted for a simpler, more utilitarian setting and ceremony.

Our denomination evolved from the Western tradition of Christianity, following Catholicism through the Protestant Reformation and the Free

Church movement. As a result, we have embraced a pragmatic, stripped-down approach to worship gatherings in which ceremony, ritual and beauty are often neglected or made secondary.

MEDIEVAL WORSHIP (AD 500–1500)

Because of the strong influence of Western Christian history on us, we will follow the Western evolution of worship through the medieval period. This period saw a significant increase in uniformity and rigidity in worship services. As the marriage of Church and State was consummated throughout the Roman Empire, churches throughout the empire were increasingly expected to embrace the Roman church's rites in every detail.

In addition to this uniformity, significant developments in theology contributed to changes in both the setting and meaning of worship practices. Sadly, these developments were often not faithful to Scripture. Instead, an increasing syncretism with surrounding mystery religions led to major changes in the meaning—though not always the method—of worship. Latin was retained as the language of the Mass, despite inroads throughout the world where Latin was not spoken. As a result, many of those who attended Christian worship services ceased to understand what was being said or what they were doing there.

Worship was increasingly seen as an epiphany (i.e. a revelation of God) wherein the work of God in communion was emphasized over the role of the worshipper. This emphasis was accompanied by an increasing confusion of signs and substance. The end result was that the Eucharist was eventually considered to be an actual sacrifice of Jesus Christ's literal body and spilling of His literal blood. Because the priest was "offering" this sacrifice, there was an increased emphasis on the active role of the minister and the passive role of the congregation. The minister performed sacraments that conveyed God's grace; the congregation received God's grace through the church.

During this time, the monastic movement evolved as a corrective against the changes taking place in the church. This movement emphasized separation from the world in reaction to an increasingly worldly church. Among the monks and nuns of this era, devotional habits were emphasized. Genuine personal and corporate spirituality through spiritual disciplines of simplicity, solitude, poverty, fasting, prayer and study were favored over the increasingly mystical, opulent, and sacrament-centric worship practices of the larger church.

While we might think of ourselves as very distant from this era in time and approach to worship, the effects have trickled down to us. We continue in a tradition that often equates the word *minister* with *pastor*, rather than acknowledging all Christians as ministers. That the problem goes deeper than our language is obvious in the active roles pastors are expected to play in service to oftentimes passive congregations.

Another practice we have unwittingly inherited from this dark era in Church history is our tradition in the Church of God (Seventh Day) of receiving the Lord's Supper only once a year. While Scripture does not dictate how often we are to receive communion, the practice of Christians from the NT up through the fourth century was to do so frequently. It was during the medieval period that the Church gradually reduced the frequency of the Eucharist from weekly to only occasional times throughout the year, or in some cases, only once a year.

Nonetheless, we have also inherited some good from this era. The monastic movement continues to influence us positively in our embrace of personal piety, our commitment to genuine spirituality and our acknowledgment of the benefit of the spiritual disciplines. We also inherited their disapproval of churches that exchange relevant teachings for mysterious platitudes spoken in unknown languages and the simplicity of the gospel for opulent cathedrals led by charlatans.

REFORMATION (AD 1517–1600)

During the tumultuous years that would later be called the Protestant Reformation, changes in theology inevitably produced changes in worship. Driving these changes was a desire to return to practices of Scripture and the early church. This included a call to re-emphasize the Table in reaction against Catholic abuses of the Mass. There was also a desire to re-emphasize the Word in reaction against illiterate and inaccessible teaching. The restoration of the balance of Word and Table in worship was central to the Reformation's impact on worship.

The impact of the Reformation on us cannot be overstated. It is from this movement that we are emboldened to depart from Roman Catholicism and instead choose another path for faith and practice. It is from this movement that we are called to Scripture as our sole authority. It is because of the Protestant Reformation that our identity is wrapped up in *protesting* impure teachings in an effort to *reform* the church.

Of the Reformers, the one whose teachings have had the greatest impact on our denominational practices was Swiss Reformer Ulrich Zwingli. It is his symbolic/memorial view of communion that our church has adopted. Along with this understanding of communion came an emphasis on the Word over the Table that is evident in our practice. While communion is shared just once a year, preaching from the Word is prioritized as the central feature of our worship service every week.

FREE CHURCH MOVEMENT (AD 1600–1900)

Perhaps more than any other period in Christian history, the Church of God (Seventh Day) has been shaped by the paradigm shifts that occurred during the Free Church era. Three major shifts occurred in the Free Church worship tradition: the anti-liturgical movement, pedagogical worship, and evangelistic worship. A few features of each of these shifts are worth noting.

The anti-liturgical movement included a rejection of set forms, ceremonies, prayer books, and lectionaries. In place of these standardized forms of worship was an emphasis on internal, "spiritual" worship and experience versus outward displays, symbols, postures, etc. This movement was accompanied by a focus on individual, private experience versus the corporate enactment of the gospel in worship. There was an overriding insistence on spontaneity over scripted worship. This became evident particularly in spontaneous prayers and extemporaneous preaching.

The shift toward pedagogical worship was marked by a focus on preaching and teaching of the Word as the central act of corporate worship. Preaching, and group Bible study, increasingly consisted of a "commentary" approach in which Scripture was read and then explained. The pedagogical shift rejected ceremony or elements of worship that appealed to the senses. Instead, they developed a simplified, text-based system of learning.

The final shift in this era, evangelistic worship, consisted of an emphasis on inward personal experience of conversion through private faith decision versus external initiation into Christ's body through baptism. The focus of worship was on conversion of the individual sinner and ongoing reformation of the individual Christian with less attention paid to corporate experience and growth.

The rich tradition of hymnody was born and thrived during this time. Hymns became a vital part of evangelistic services as many hymns sought to call sinners to salvation and believers to revival. Interestingly, when hymns were first introduced, they were initially rejected and treated with skepticism by most established churches. Nonetheless, within churches that utilized them, hymns added to the evangelistic flavor of preaching that was aimed at effecting change in the listener.

Many hymns were aimed at attracting individuals to the "altar" to experience a work of grace. This marked an interesting transition from the practice of Catholicism. Within Catholic churches, the front of the meeting space was called an "altar" because it was there that the priest offered the "sacrifice" of the Eucharist. Congregants would kneel there to receive grace through the taking of communion. Within free churches of the Protestant movement, the kneeling rail itself became the "altar" upon which individual parishioners were expected to offer themselves sacrificially to God.

As noted before, this era of church history has had a dramatic impact on our denomination's worship practices. We have inherited the rejection of most historic liturgy and set forms in favor of improvised liturgies and spontaneous prayers and preaching. We have adopted a pedagogical approach to Bible reading and study, anticipating that preachers and teachers will read Scripture and comment on it in order to provide the proper interpretation to the audience. Finally, we have adopted the practice of singing hymns—and now modern choruses—as part of an effort to reach both sinners and saints with a message of individual conversion and spiritual growth.

TWENTIETH CENTURY RENEWAL MOVEMENTS (AD 1900-2000)

The final era of Christian worship brings us to the modern day as we look at the twentieth century. Three major movements stand out in this era.

The first was the Azusa Street Revivals from 1906-1908 in Los Angeles, California. With its full display of the gifts of the Spirit and thousands of participants drawn from around the world, this revival marked a turning point in church history. These revivals gave birth to the historic Pentecostal denominations known to us today, including the Foursquare Church, the Assemblies of God and the Church of God in Christ. As these denominations grew, they began to exercise influence within the body of Christ, resulting in the second major event.

The Charismatic Renewal Movement (1960s–1970s) involved the spread of prophecy, speaking in tongues, healings, and miracles into mainline churches. Whereas the Azusa Street Revivals saw individuals leaving their denominations to join newly formed Pentecostal churches, the Charismatic renewal was marked by individuals experiencing the full range of the gifts of the Spirit, but choosing to remain in their non-Pentecostal churches. This choice allowed the gifts of the Spirit and the unique Pentecostal form of worship to influence all Protestant denominations and even the Catholic Church.

Following this initial renewal, historians observed what is called the Third Wave (1980s–present). Most trace its origins to Vineyard Church founder John Wimber and the emphasis on healing versus speaking in tongues, and on worship as an environment in which God ministers directly to people through His Spirit. Pentecostalism, the Charismatic Renewal, and the Third Wave together contributed to the evolution of a Charismatic worship style.

This style is marked by a "planned spontaneity" in which great efforts are made to welcome the Holy Spirit as an active participant in the worship service by carefully creating the right atmosphere, while maintaining freedom for extemporaneous prayers, singing, prophetic utterances, miracles, etc. The creation of this "atmosphere" includes a focus on progressing from "praise" to "worship." In this model, "praise" is characterized by speed, volume, energy, joy, shouting, clapping, and dancing, while "worship" is characterized by slower pacing, lower volume, subdued mood, conviction/reflection/adoration, murmured prayer, raising hands, and kneeling.

In the Charismatic worship style, there is a focus on spiritual gifting and the talent of musicians and singers leading the congregation in participatory worship. This participation is encouraged throughout the service in inspired utterance, prayer, response, dance, drama, etc. Time is set aside after the sermon for ministry at the altar. Worshipers are invited forward to sing, kneel, pray, etc., and be ministered to through healing, prophecy, prayer, etc.

To varying degrees, the effects of Charismatic worship can be observed throughout our denomination. Some of our congregations are fully Pentecostal in their belief and practice related to the Holy Spirit and the gifts. Their worship style is shaped almost entirely by the style developed in the past one hundred years. On the other end of the spectrum we have congregations that have attempted to reject this approach altogether. Most of our congregations land somewhere between these poles. The Charismatic style influences many of our churches in terms of our desire to be led by gifted singers/musicians, our commitment to congregational participation, our interest in inviting the Holy Spirit to minister to us, and the distinctions we often make between "praise" and "worship" songs.

CONCLUSION

In this brief review we've seen that much of our understanding and practice of worship is shaped by traditions passed on from various eras in church history. We ought to embrace this reality and give careful attention to the traditions we've inherited. Perhaps we have embraced practices that should be reconsidered in the light of Scripture and church history. Perhaps we have failed to embrace other practices out of fear or misinformation. Let us listen closely to the lessons of history and learn from them as we pass our understanding and practice of worship on to the next generation.

REVIEW QUESTIONS

1. What is the significance of studying history as it relates to developing a theology and practice of worship? List three insights.

2. What are the three major eras of Western Christian history?

3. What are five features that characterize worship in each of the major eras of Christian history?

APPLICATION QUESTIONS

1. What are the current liturgy and expectations of your local church congregation?

2. Compare and contrast our modern worship with New Testament worship. What is the same? What is different? Are our goals and focus the same?

3. Reviewing the features that characterize worship in each era of Christian history, what are the sources of your congregation's current theology and practice of worship?

4. Identify at least five practices that your congregation has inherited through tradition, rather than directly from Scripture.

5. Consider the practices you just listed. How do they relate to Scripture?

6. Identify at least three historical practices that your congregation has not embraced, perhaps because of fear or misinformation. Reevaluate these practices in light of Scripture.

Endnotes

Scripture quotations are from the *New American Standard Bible*.

1. Robert E. Webber, *Worship: Old & New Revised Edition* (Grand Rapids: Zondervan, 1994), 93–134.
2. Ibid., 93–94.

CHAPTER 8

TRUE WORSHIP ACCORDING TO JESUS

The only "worship is" statement found in the New Testament was made by Jesus during His encounter with the Samaritan woman. True worship, according to Jesus, is worship which is done in spirit and in truth.

After reading this chapter, you will be able to

- distinguish between the *mode* and *manner* of worship;
- identify the role of the revelation of God in worship;
- define the phrase "worship in spirit and truth";
- define *transactional worship*.

True worship involves the whole person, mind, heart, body, and spirit. This is Psalm 103 worship: "Bless the Lord, O my soul, and all that is within me, bless His holy name."

Martin Luther is reported to have said, "God gave us five senses with which to worship Him, and it would be sheer ingratitude for us to worship Him with less."

Hear, O Israel: The Lord our God, the Lord is one! You shall love the Lord your God with all your heart, with all your soul, and with all your strength (Deuteronomy 6:4, 5).

The familiar story of Jesus' encounter with the woman at the well of Samaria can serve as a guide to understanding biblical worship. Jesus' comment about the woman's past made her uncomfortable, so she decided to change the subject. Her reaction has been described as "the universal reflex of people trying to avoid conviction."[1] And since Samaritans and Jews disagree over the acceptable place of worship (shall it be Mount Gerazim or on Jerusalem's holy mount?), she shifted the conversation to that topic: "Our fathers worshiped on this mountain, and you Jews say that in Jerusalem is the place where one ought to worship" (John 4:20).

Different versions of this question have remained at the heart of "worship wars" for centuries. Today we ask, "What constitutes true worship? Which is the right way to worship: traditional or contemporary, hymns or choruses, high church or free style?"

Jesus took no sides in that debate, but rather offered a radically different worship paradigm: "Woman, believe Me, the hour is coming when you will neither on this mountain, nor in Jerusalem, worship the Father. You worship what you do not know; we know what we worship, for salvation is of the Jews. But the hour is coming, and now is, when the true worshipers will worship the Father in spirit and truth; for the Father is seeking such to worship

Him. God is Spirit, and those who worship Him must worship in spirit and truth" (John 4:21–24).

For context, it should be noted that tension between Samaritans and Jews was centuries old. The Assyrians (Babylon) conquered Israel and took many of its people (mainly the chiefs and nobles) into captivity in 722 bc. The invaders then sent colonists to resettle the land (2 Kings 17:24), which resulted in intermarriages between these Assyrians and those Jews who were left behind, which eventually resulted in the mixture of true and false worship (2 Kings 17:29–41; Ezra 9:1-10:44). This also resulted in a new race of people called Samaritans, who were detested by full-blooded Jews. The Samaritans did not embrace the entire Old Testament and recognized a separate place of worship that goes all the way back to the "rival sanctuary" established when the kingdom divided after the death of Solomon. Walls of bitterness and separation were therefore built by both groups, which had only hardened over the next five-plus centuries, up to the time of Jesus. The question of the proper place of worship was therefore a subject of hot debate between Samaritans and Jews, fueled by deep emotion.

With that background in mind, let us consider Jesus' response to the woman regarding the right place of worship. The following two words can be helpful in understanding Jesus's answer: *mode* and *manner*. *Mode* refers to style, culture, and personality, for which the Bible allows much latitude. *Manner*, on the other hand, refers to substance, content, which is standard and derived from Scripture. By calling attention to the biblical orientation of Samaritans and Jews—Samaritans worship what they do not know, Jews worship what they do know—Jesus directs His comments to the manner of worship (its biblical content and substance), rather than the mode of worship (style, personal preference, etc.).

In other words, the identifying mark of true worship is no longer right location, no longer about this or that place, the Jerusalem temple or a religious shrine. What, then, is true worship? Jesus declared, "But the hour is coming, and now is, when the true worshipers will worship the Father in spirit and truth; for the Father is seeking such to worship Him. God is Spirit, and those who worship Him must worship in spirit and truth." Therefore, true worship, according to Jesus, is worship that is in spirit and in truth.

IN SPIRIT

The term "in spirit" has been variously interpreted. A common understanding is that this is a reference to our human spirit, our inner being, heart, mind, soul—not to the Holy Spirit. This view is supported by the fact that the s in *spirit* is lowercase.

Another understanding is that "in spirit" means passionately, from the heart, with all that is within us. This has been called "Psalm 103 worship": "Bless the Lord, O my soul, and all that is within me, bless His holy name" (v. 1). That is the focus of the Shema: "Hear, O Israel: The Lord our God, the Lord is one! You shall love the Lord your God with all your heart, with all your soul, and with all your strength" (Deuteronomy 6:4, 5). The most basic expression of that kind of love for God is worship. That's why God's biggest complaint against Israel's worship through the centuries was their lack of heart: "These people draw near to Me with their mouth, and honor Me with their lips, but their heart is far from Me" (Isaiah 29:13; Matthew 15:8). So to worship "in spirit" is to do so passionately, from the heart, with all that's within us, inwardly, the opposite of doing so outwardly in external conformity to religious ritual.

But there's yet another consideration as to the meaning of this term. "In spirit" in John 4 where Jesus introduces the Samaritan woman to the water of salvation should not be divorced from "the spirit" in John 3 where Jesus tells Nicodemus that to have eternal life one must be born of "the spirit." In John 3, Jesus is obviously not speaking of human spirit. To be born again is to be born of the Holy Spirit, meaning supernaturally, not of the flesh or human origin, but of God. This third view of "in spirit" is that while it doesn't mean Holy Spirit, it certainly means more than human spirit. To worship "in spirit" is to worship under the inspiration and influence of the supernatural.

IN TRUTH

But Jesus also said that true worship must be in truth. Worship is universal in its appeal and practice, meaning that all peoples and cultures worship. But not all worship is acceptable to God. A Hindu offering up rice patties as a form of worship is not true worship. The worship God desires, the worship He accepts, is that which begins with the truth about Him, a right understanding of who He is, His divine nature and self-revelation. True worship is our heart response to God's revelation about Himself through creation, the written Word, the Bible, and the living Word, the Lord Jesus Christ. Jesus is the truth (John 14:6), the greatest truth we can know, which makes Him the centerpiece of true worship.

Worship that flows from the combination of these two essentials—"spirit and truth"—is balanced worship. It engages heart and head, emotion and thought. The old axiom is true: "All spirit and no truth, people blow up; all truth and no spirit, people dry up; spirit and truth in balance, people grow up." Said in a different way, spirit without truth leads to fanaticism (mindless frenzy); truth without spirit leads to legalism (dead orthodoxy). Spirit and truth in balance equals true worship.

A BEAUTIFUL STORY

Jesus stopped by the well that day, not just because He was tired, but because He had a divine appointment. The Father is actively seeking people who will worship Him, and He seeks them among the weary and wounded, the least worthy. John's commentary that this encounter took place at noon (v. 6) is not incidental. It was quite uncommon in that day to find a woman at the well at noon, but not if you were a Samaritan woman. She came at noon because she was an outcast—on three counts: She was a woman, she was a Samaritan, and she was divorced. She therefore lived on the fringes of society, and religious tradition had done nothing to ease the pain of her five broken marriages: "for you have had five husbands, and the one whom you now have is not your husband" (v. 18). So there in a quiet place beside Jacob's well, Jesus introduced her to a different kind of water, one that meets the deepest need of the human heart.

The story ends with the woman running back to the village to call her neighbors to come see the Man who changed her life. At this point John makes another insightful commentary – that in running back to the village, she left her water jar behind (v. 28). A water jar was a valuable thing to own in that day and culture. Water is critical to our physical existence and domestic needs, and back in that day having a container in which to carry it was no small matter. But at this point in the story, the Samaritan woman is caught up with something she considered much more valuable. True worship is to recklessly abandon all we are and have in exchange for the all-surpassing joy of knowing and following Jesus. She had gone to the well to draw water, and Jesus gave her something much better—"a revolution of the heart." She now had a heart set free to live the life for which she was created. When we discover the truth about who God is, we also discover the truth about ourselves, our origin, identity, and destiny. Worship involves the discovery of life's true meaning and purpose and then living "coram deo," before the face of God. It is exposing our heart to the one who knows everything about us—"come see a Man who told me all things that I ever did" (v. 29). It is having a life-changing encounter with the incomparable Christ. Such was the Samaritan woman's experience. Such is true worship.

REVIEW QUESTIONS

1. What is the difference between the *mode* and *manner* of worship? Which of these did Jesus emphasize in His conversation with the Samaritan woman?

2. What is the role of the revelation of God in worship?

3. What does it mean to "worship in spirit and truth"?

APPLICATION QUESTIONS

1. Jesus directed His comments toward the biblical content and substance (mode) of the Samaritans' worship. What are some ways in which you justify elevating personal preference (manner) in worship?

2. Even though both the Jews and the Samaritans worshipped the same God, *Yahweh*, Jesus emphasized that the Jews worshipped a God they knew while the Samaritans worshipped a God they did not know. How do you currently maintain an awareness of the character and desires of Yahweh?

3. Inward worship engages the mind, beginning with "truth about Him, a right understanding of who He is, His divine nature and self-revelation." How are you engaging your mind in worship?

4. Inward worship also engages our hearts as we respond to "God's revelation about Himself through creation, the written Word, and the Living Word." How are you engaging your heart in worship?

5. "Emotion" and "intellect" are often viewed as opposing approaches to worship, yet true worship engages both heart and head, both emotion and thought. Which of these approaches do you gravitate toward? Why? How might you achieve more balance in this area?

6. To live "coram deo"—before the face of God—is to "expose our heart to the one who knows everything about us." How does living coram deo make us more aware of our own tendencies toward transactional worship (see Chapter 5)?

Endnotes

Scripture quotations were taken from the *New King James Version.*

1. John Piper, *Desiring God, Revised Edition* (Colorado Springs: Multnomah Books, 2011), 64.

CHAPTER 9

MUSIC IN WORSHIP

Worship isn't music, but understanding the power and impact of music can assist and enhance both private and corporate worship.

After reading this chapter, you will be able to

- explain why worship leaders should handle music selection with care and wisdom;
- identify two ways in which worship leaders can handle music selection with care and wisdom;
- give three examples of how culture influenced Christian music before the twentieth century;
- describe the likely distinction between "psalms, hymns, and spiritual songs";
- identify the defining characteristics of each era of Christian music.

Let the word of Christ dwell in you richly in all wisdom, teaching and admonishing one another in psalms and hymns and spiritual songs, singing with grace in your hearts to the Lord (Colossians 3:16).

And do not be drunk with wine, in which is dissipation; but be filled with the Spirit, speaking to one another in psalms and hymns and spiritual songs, singing and making melody in your heart to the Lord (Ephesians 5:18, 19).

Praise the Lord!

Praise God in His sanctuary;
Praise Him in His mighty firmament!

Praise Him for His mighty acts;
Praise Him according to His excellent greatness!

Praise Him with the sound of the trumpet;
Praise Him with the lute and harp!

Praise Him with the timbrel and dance;
Praise Him with stringed instruments and flutes!

Praise Him with loud cymbals;
Praise Him with clashing cymbals!

Let everything that has breath praise the Lord.

Praise the Lord (Psalm 150).

"Music's only purpose should be the glory of God and the recreation of the human spirit."[1]

"...a character should sing when the emotion has become too high for ordinary speech."[2]

Much is at stake when a pastor or worship team sets out to select music for a worship service. It is often noted that worship isn't music. That is to say, that music is not a fundamental element of worship; one can worship without music. But music can greatly assist and enhance private and corporate worship. That is likely the reason there's a hymnbook (the Psalms, the Hebrew Psalter) in the middle of our Bible, replete with invitations to sing and play instruments of praise, to make music to the Lord. And beyond the Psalms, the pages of Scripture testify to the importance and power of song: "Let the word of Christ dwell in you richly in all wisdom, teaching and admonishing one another in psalms and hymns and spiritual songs, singing with grace in your hearts to the Lord" (Colossians 3:16).

Because Scripture places such a high premium on music, because music is powerful and stirs the emotion like no other art form, because music has the power to unite and divide, worship leaders should handle music selection with much care and wisdom. They should have a working knowledge of the history of music in the Bible and the Christian church. They should have a sincere appreciation for both traditional and contemporary musical genres and be committed to finding ways to "incorporate both the richness and dignity of the hymns of the church with the inspiration and relevance of gospel songs and contemporary choruses."

For a quick overview of the history of music in Scripture and Christian history, we turn to *Worship Old and New*, by the late Robert E. Webber, in the chapter titled "The Role of Music in Worship."[3]

Music's central place in Christian liturgy is rooted in Old Testament Scripture. Hebrew culture was shaped as much by its music as it was by the law, which made music central to the worship of the early New Testament church.

Music evolved simultaneously with the growth and development of the church and its liturgy. By the fourth and fifth centuries a more elaborate style of music known as "responsorial psalm" took shape, in which psalms were sung by a soloist and the congregation responded at the end of each verse. The view later developed that the church should sing only psalms, since they were God's inspired Word, a view still held by some in our day. But not everyone during that era shared that view, evidenced by church leaders such as Ambrose (Bishop of Milan), who wrote and compiled a large collection of church music.

THE MEDIEVAL ERA

The medieval era saw significant progress as well as unfortunate developments. Some of the most beautiful music ever written in the history of the Christian church was written during this era and spread throughout the West. But it was also during this era that singing by lay people was banned.

MEDIEVAL ERA HYMNS

All Glory, Laud, and Honor
Jesus, the Very Thought of Thee
O Sacred Head Now Wounded
The Gregorian Chants

THE REFORMATION

Much more was accomplished in the interest of worship and music by the sixteenth century Reformation than many realize. Luther believed that the Reformation was incomplete until God's people had two books in their possession: the Bible-book and the hymnbook. With the Bible-book they would learn the truths about God and His plan of salvation, and with the hymn book they would respond in worship. For the end goal of theology, someone has wisely said, is doxology. Therefore, because Luther was a trained musician and hymn writer and had a heart for composing music for the common people, the history of the Reformation is marked both by commitment to the Word of God and the music that proceeds from it. As Luther's Reformation theology spread throughout the West like wildfire, so did its music.

THE GRAND HYMN OF THE REFORMATION

A Mighty Fortress Is Our God

But a century later, the music of the church needed renewal. This is known as the modern era, and its renewal is largely credited to "the father of modern hymnody," Isaac Watts. He had become disenchanted with the music of the church as a young man and was challenged by his father to do something about it. This inspired him to compose a hymn for the following week, which he did, followed by weekly compositions, eventually numbering more than six hundred. The eighteenth century composer was soon joined by John and Charles Wesley. But their hymns took on a notable shift in focus from the objective (God-centered) to subjective experience due to the revival emphasis of the Wesleys and the Methodist movement. And yet it should be noted that although the songs of this period were more subjective, "they still retained a healthy objective emphasis on God."[4]

HYMNS OF THE MODERN ERA

Love Divine, All Loves Excelling
The God of Abraham Praise
All Hail the Power of Jesus' Name
Glorious Things of Thee Are Spoken

THE GOSPEL ERA

This paved the way for the emergence of "gospel songs" in the nineteenth century, which facilitated the mass evangelistic efforts of the likes of D. L. Moody and revival preachers. The most noted writer of gospel songs of that era was Fanny Crosby who, though blind from birth, wrote thousands of such songs and gained much notoriety during the formative years of the United States.

SONGS OF THE GOSPEL ERA

Rescue the Perishing
Just As I Am
Take My Life and Let It Be

THE TWENTIETH CENTURY

The connection between music and culture becomes more and more apparent as we move into the twentieth century. Those who've studied this note that two World Wars, a Civil War, and a major economic downturn here at home had profound influence on the sound and feel of music, resulting in the emergence of a new musical form known as "pop music," a term that references the popular music of the culture, "transmitted via mass media and aimed particularly at younger people." Add to this the emergence of the Pentecostal and Charismatic movements in the early nineteen hundreds and the coming of age of the United States in the sixties, accompanied by the Jesus movement, and the result is a drastic reshaping of the country's music landscape. Worship choruses are introduced for the first time, the use of the word "entertainment" in relation to Christian worship becomes vogue, and the notion that new converts should be allowed to bring their musical tastes and styles with them to church, were part of the new musical evolution.

CULTURE AND MUSIC

Not surprisingly, there's debate and even division over whether or not this is even appropriate. Should culture be reflected in the music and worship of the church? The reality is that the influence of culture on Christian music and worship is unavoidable. Ron Moore notes that "Every song we sing was written by a person of a particular era, for people of that era, in the style of that era, borrowed from the music of that era." This has been true throughout church history—from the baroque era to the time of the Reformation to the present. A classic example is the well-known hymn of the Reformation, "A Mighty Fortress Is Our God" (based on Psalm 46), the words of which were set to the music of a popular bar tune of that day. This likely caused no little furor within the German church. But the irony is that a hymn that was obviously viewed back in the 1600s as way too cultural and contemporary is now viewed by many in the modern church of our day as way too traditional.

The question therefore isn't whether or not culture should influence the music of the church; that is a given. Rather, the question is how can the church influence the way culture influences its music? It can by developing a biblical theology of worship and by cultivating an environment that appreciates all that God has given to the church in terms of music throughout its history. This facilitates greater diversity in music, bringing together the traditional and contemporary models. There are negative consequences to a steady diet on the same type of music. Webber writes, "An *exclusive* use of Christian pop choruses cuts the church off from the treasuries of Christian music given to the church throughout the centuries. However, choruses, like gospel music or other forms of music given to the church, should not be excluded from worship but incorporated at the appropriate places in worship and added to the use of hymns, psalms, and other musical forms."[5] This approach is commonly known as "blended worship."

AN IMPORTANT CAUTION

Given the fact that we cannot prevent the influence of culture on the music of the church, the following additional commentary is necessary to safeguard against the notion that there is no objective standard by which to judge which music is acceptable for the worship of God and which is not. There is good music and there is bad music. Theologians like to remind us that music is a "common grace," meaning that it is a gift from God given to all people—the just and the unjust. Believers are to approach music as God's gift to be used as an expression of their love for Him and gratitude for His redemption through Christ. But unbelievers do not share such commitment. Paul understands the difference, which is why he leads into his comments on the use of music in worship by contrasting drunkenness with Spirit fullness: "And do not be drunk with wine, in which is dissipation; but be filled with the Spirit, speaking to one another in psalms and hymns and spiritual songs, singing and making melody in your heart to the Lord" (Ephesians 5:18, 19). In ancient pagan religion it was believed that the way to connect with the gods was to lose control, to work oneself into a frenzy, to become drunk, and in some cases, to indulge in sensuality and sexual orgies. As Christians, we need not lose control in order to connect with the supernatural; the supernatural indwells us. Music that is given to working oneself into a frenzy in an effort to connect with God is bad music. What makes music good or bad is what drives and motivates it. Good music gives expression to the unchangeable reality of God's nature and affirms the truth of His Word.

NEGRO SPIRITUALS AND GOSPEL

Finally, something needs to be said about spirituals and gospel, so here's a quick summary. By the mid-1800s there were several million Africans in the United States, uprooted from their homeland and brought to this country against their will to live as slaves. But their circumstances didn't diminish their rich heritage of soul and song; it actually increased it. Out of this experience emerged a new musical form known as "spirituals," songs that reflected their difficult circumstances through lament, protest, and quest for freedom. Dr. Martin Luther King, leader of the Civil Rights Movement of the 1960s, affectionately called them "freedom songs." Dr. James Norris of Howard University notes that these songs were everything to the enslaved Africans; singing was how they maintained their sanity and remained hopeful. In her book *A Cup of Sun*, poet Joan Walsh Anglund asserts, "A bird doesn't sing because it has an answer, it sings because it has a song."[6] The African slaves had a song, and they couldn't help but sing it. It was the music of their soul, the one thing that could not be taken away from them.

Students of African American history tell us that plantation owners often made their slaves attend church to listen to the message of Christianity. Despite their inability to read and write and the religious customs out of which they came, these slaves quickly and creatively began composing songs based on the biblical narrative, often using coded language to give expression to their pain and desire for comfort ("There is a Balm in Gilead"), being homesick for their motherland ("Sometimes I Feel Like a Motherless Child, a Long Way From Home"), hope for a better life ("Deep River"), and even their visions of escape ("Steal Away Home" and "Swing Low, Sweet Chariot"). The lyrics of these songs were rooted in the biblical text, but to the enslaved Africans, the meaning of these words and their application were deeply personal.

This finds support in the following statement found in the introduction to the hymnal *Songs of Zion*, "The Negro Spirituals...are the most beautiful expression of human experience born this side of the seas."[7] Regarding their powerful impact, one writer notes, "...what gives Negro spiritual songs their power is the way in which they invite the human voice to add contour, rhythm, texture, melody, tempo, variation, and emotional depth to words. The African-American experience resonates within and all through them."[8]

Other forms and styles of music popular in our day that emerged from the spirituals include the blues, jazz, hip hop and, last but not least, black gospel, made popular by twentieth century composers such as Thomas A. Dorsey and others. Though the personal experiences that drove black gospel music were different from those that drove the spirituals, their pathos and rhythm are no less powerful.

MUSIC IN GENERAL

Music is often described as one of the most divisive elements in the life and ministry of the church. While there's truth to that statement, that isn't the whole truth about music. It is one of the most divisive elements in the church for the same reason it is one of God's best gifts to the church and humanity. Nothing stirs the emotions and penetrates the human spirit quite like it. Music can calm the soul, settle the mind, and gladden the heart. In fact, there's a research study which shows that music is the only art form that affects the nervous system. It's been called the universal language and the food of life. It is no easier to try to imagine a world without sunlight than to try to imagine a world without music. That's why theologians call it "a gift of common grace" given to all humanity.

But we can be sure that sin's corrupting influence on the world has affected music, giving the redeemed a considerable hedge when it comes to music that honors God. The oft repeated admonition from the Psalm to "Sing to Him a new song" (Psalm 33:3) has been taken by some to mean that we must not sing the same songs over and over again. But a more accurate understanding of the word "new" is a reference to the song the redeemed now sing versus the old songs we used to sing. The redeemed of the Lord have been given a new song which we alone can sing: "He has put a new song in my mouth—a song of praise to our God" (Psalm 40:3). Indeed, as someone has said, "Music finds its highest purpose when used as a tool to extol the greatness of God."

This explains why Paul's admonition to sing psalms, hymns and spiritual songs in Ephesians 5 is preceded by these words: "And do not be drunk with wine, in which is dissipation; but be filled with the Spirit" (v. 18). To be drunk with wine is to be under its influence; to be filled with the Spirit is to be under the Spirit's control. Those who practiced ancient pagan religion believed that in order to connect and communicate with the gods they needed to lose control of themselves, to engage in drunken and even sexual orgies. Paul wanted the Ephesian Christians to understand that this isn't necessary, that we don't do that. Rather, believers are to be filled with the Spirit, demonstrated by worship adorned by psalms, hymns and spiritual songs with which they make melody (music) to the Lord.

What, then, are psalms, hymns and spiritual songs, terms twice repeated by Paul in Ephesians and Colossians? Psalms likely refer to the Hebrew Psalter found in the middle of our Bible. This rich collection of songs written under the inspiration of the Holy Spirit has had wide appeal among believers down through time because these songs assist our praise of the greatness and glory of God (the Hebrew word Psalm means praise) while at the same time reflecting the full gamut of our human emotions. Hymns seem to be distinct from Psalms in that while they aren't part of the inspired canon, they nonetheless reflect the doctrinal truths of salvation and the theological foundations of the Judeo Christian heritage. The classic hymns have a depth of wisdom and biblical content that is unique. Hymns were apparently part of Jewish liturgy, because after the Last Supper Jesus and His disciples sang a hymn before leaving the Upper Room (Matthew 26:30; Mark 14:26). The term "spiritual songs," therefore, has in mind a broader range of songs based on spiritual themes that express personal testimony of salvation (such as John Newton's "Amazing Grace"), provision, or deliverance, etc. They encompass the music of the redeemed, which we will sing long after the music of the world has ceased. Yes, one day the world's music will cease: "Then a mighty angel took up a stone like a great millstone and threw it into the sea, saying, "Thus with violence the great city Babylon shall be thrown down, and shall not be found anymore. The sound of harpists, musicians, flutists, and trumpeters shall not be heard in you anymore" (Revelation 18:21, 22), but the music of the redeemed will never end because we worship Him who lives forever and ever (Revelation 5:14).

> When we've been there ten thousand years,
> Bright shining as the sun,
> We've no less days to sing God's praise
> Than when we first begun.

REVIEW QUESTIONS

1. Why should worship leaders handle music selection with care and wisdom?

2. What are two ways in which worship leaders handle music selection with care and wisdom?

3. What are three examples of how culture influenced Christian music before the twentieth century?

4. What is the likely distinction between "psalms, hymns, and spiritual songs"?

5. What are the defining characteristics of each era of Christian music?

APPLICATION QUESTIONS

1. How does a biblical theology of worship cultivate an environment that appreciates all that God has given to the church in terms of music throughout its history?

2. What has God given to the church in terms of music in each of the eras studied?

3. How does diversity of music facilitate worship?

4. How does an understanding of what God has given to the church in terms of music in each of the eras studied enrich your worship of Him?

Endnotes

Scripture quotations were taken from the *New King James Version*.

1. Johann Sebastian Bach, quoted in "J. S. Bach: For the Glory of God," *Christianity Today*, October 14, 2005 (http://www.christianitytoday.com/ct/2005/octoberweb-only/52.0a.html). Web accessed 9-8-15.

2. Quote attributed to Oscar Hammerstein (http://www.musicalwriters.com/write/stephen-schwartz/musicals/music-lyrics.htm). Web accessed 9-14-15.

3. Robert E. Webber, *Worship: Old & New Revised Edition* (Grand Rapids: Zondervan, 1994), 195–203.

4. Ibid., 200.

5. Ibid., 201.

6. Joan Walsh Anglund, *A Cup of Sun* (Harcourt, Brace & World, 1967), 15. According to several sources, this quote has been misattributed to Maya Angelo in her book *I Know Why the Caged Bird Sings* (https://www.washingtonpost.com/lifestyle/style/lonnae-oneal-a-possible-misquote-that-may-last-forever/2015/04/04/41f937a4-da3c-11e4-b3f2-607bd612aeac_story.html). Web accessed 9-8-15.

7. J. Jefferson Cleveland in collaboration with William B. McClain, *Songs of Zion* (Nashville: Abington Press, 1981), 73.

8. "Why 'Negro Spiritual,'" The "Negro Spiritual" Scholarship Foundation (http://www.negrospiritual.org/why-negro-spiritual). Web accessed 9-8-15.

CHAPTER 10

FINDING BALANCE (PART 1)
TRADITIONAL VERSUS CONTEMPORARY

Division in the body of Christ over worship grieves the Spirit of God. The task before this generation is to bridge this divide through worship that is balanced, that brings together the best elements of both traditional and contemporary worship.

After reading this chapter, you will be able to

- describe the significance of diversity in the body of Christ on worship;
- compare and contrast the *manner* and *mode of worship*;
- define the word *traditional*;
- define the word *contemporary*;

- compare and contrast tradition and traditionalism;
- define *blended worship*.

"Tradition is the living faith of the dead, traditionalism is the dead faith of the living."[1]

"We evangelicals do not know much about worship. Evangelism is our specialty, not worship. We have little sense of the greatness of Almighty God. We tend to be cocky, flippant, and proud. And our worship services are often ill-prepared, slovenly, mechanical, perfunctory, and dull.... Much of our public worship is ritual without reality, form without power, religion without God."[2]

Now I praise you, brethren, that you remember me in all things and keep the traditions just as I delivered them to you (1 Corinthians 11:2).

And I advanced in Judaism beyond many of my contemporaries in my own nation, being more exceedingly zealous for the traditions of my fathers (Galatians 1:14).

Therefore, brethren, stand fast and hold the traditions which you were taught, whether by word or our epistle (2 Thessalonians 2:15).

And in vain they worship Me; teaching as doctrines the commandments of men (Matthew 15:9).

B alance is an essential ingredient of healthy and meaningful living. Life fares better when we balance work and rest, eat a balanced diet, and balance our checkbook. Our national economy would fare better if the government balanced the federal budget.

Balance is essential in spiritual matters as well. It's been noted that "heresy is truth out of balance"; a good teaching taken to an extreme. Believers are called to balance faith and works, spirit and truth, law and grace, the Bible-book and the hymnbook. And finding balance is the secret to ending many a worship war. This and the following chapters are therefore devoted to addressing the difficult yet hopeful business of finding balance in worship.

THE STARK REALITY

The first murder in the Bible resulted from a disagreement over worship. That statement is usually made as an attention getter, but it is not without biblical basis. We read in Genesis 4 that Cain and Abel offered sacrifices to the Lord. We also read that the Lord had respect to Abel and his offering, but not to Cain. That rejection evoked anger in Cain to the degree that he killed his brother (Genesis 4:1–8). Sin's corrupting influence was taking its toll on the human family, and manifested itself in a deadly conflict related to worship.

That the first murder in the Bible resulted from a disagreement over whose worship was more acceptable is no small matter. But more pressing is the fact that such disagreements have continued throughout time, and are increasingly common in our day. It's been said that worship remains one of the most divisive elements of the Christian church, so much so that over the past fifty years or so the term "worship wars" has now become a common part of the American church's lingo. Christians divide over worship, drawing battle lines in various places, and over various issues. This is no small matter. So for the purpose of this chapter we will narrow it down to two ends of the worship spectrum that are well-known and commonly discussed: traditional versus contemporary.

The traditional style is what comes to mind when an older generation of Christians think about worship. It involves a more structured and predictable format, with hymns, the reading of Scripture, and the sermon as the climax of the worship experience. On the other hand, contemporary worship usually means the organ is out (the piano, too, in some places) and the keyboard and guitar are in. Older hymns are replaced with newer worship songs; choirs replaced with praise bands; Bibles and hymnals with video screens and PowerPoint; and liturgy with free style.

Sadly, the division between these two camps has become so familiar that many in the body of Christ are no longer grieved by it. But when the church divides, the Spirit grieves, and so should God's people. The poet William Stidger had military warfare in mind when he wrote,

God cried Himself to sleep last night.
He saw ten thousand sons of His on cruel crosses slain.[3]

If God's heart is pained by the casualties of military war, imagine how much more deeply His heart is pained over the casualties of worship wars. The Spirit's call to this generation is therefore to find balance.

This is a difficult and sensitive subject, so we must proceed with caution. Obviously, not everyone in each of these camps is at the same place on that worship continuum. Each has its extreme and conservative elements, which increases the challenge of finding balance. Nonetheless, we must begin somewhere. And to help us do so, the following are offered for consideration.

THE REALITY OF DIVERSITY

The first step in finding balance is recognizing the reality of diversity within Christ's body. The gospel of Christ is a gospel for all people (Matthew 28:19), which makes the body of Christ as diverse as the people who respond to the gospel. This diversity is emphasized in New Testament scriptures such as 1 Corinthians 12 where Christ's body is shown to be diverse in its giftedness, ministries, and activities. It is also emphasized in Ephesians 4 where Paul elaborates on the various gifts Jesus distributed to His church upon His ascension. These and other references affirm that the body of Christ is very diverse, that we aren't stripped of our ethnicity and cultural and personal differences when we come to Christ. We still have varying likes and dislikes, different tastes and preferences, which results in a great deal of diversity when it comes to worship. Furthermore, the company of the redeemed in Revelation is described as being from every nation, tribe, people and language (7:9), meaning that the diversity of the church carries over into eternity. All of this leads to the conclusion that diversity is a reality of Christ's body, a reality most clearly manifested in worship. This means that differences in worship styles and preferences are to be expected. That's how God designed the church. This is the beginning point of any attempt to find balance in worship.

MANNER AND MODE

Another important consideration in finding balance in worship is the difference between what worship practitioners call the manner and mode of worship.

This is addressed elsewhere in this book, but here's a quick summary for the purpose of this chapter:

Manner refers to biblical content and substance, worship's essential ingredients, while *mode* refers to style.

Manner is standard and is based on Scripture; *mode* is subjective and is largely driven by culture and personality.

The Bible prescribes *manner*, while allowing a great deal of latitude and freedom when it comes to *mode*.

This helpful distinction affirms what has been observed over the years—that much of what Christians usually divide over when it comes to worship aren't matters prescribed in Scripture, but rather, are matters on which Scripture allows much latitude. Some Christians don't allow the latitude that Scripture allows in these areas. For instance, nothing is said in Scripture about an order of service, the length of the sermon (or even if there should be a sermon), whether or not there should be chairs or pews in a church facility, etc. When it comes to what Scripture does prescribe, two things are explicitly mentioned: worship must be in spirit and in truth (John 4:23). An entire chapter in this book is devoted to unpacking what it means to worship in spirit and in truth, but for now, we'll simply note that to worship in spirit is to engage our entire being (heart, soul, and strength, as the Shema instructs in Deuteronomy 6:4, 5), and to worship in truth is to do so in accordance with the truth of God's Word.

It is helpful to note at this point that, regarding mode, what it means to worship God in spirit will be applied differently by different people depending on personality, culture, etc. In fact, we even differ on what it means to worship in truth because of our varying interpretations of truth. So the next time a worship war looms at your church, pause to consider whether or not the issue at the heart of the conflict is manner (the biblical requirements) or mode (personal or cultural preference). More often than not, it is the latter.

THE WORDS *TRADITIONAL* AND *CONTEMPORARY*

Many a worship war results either from putting too much stock in certain words or from not fully understanding their meaning in the first place. There are Christians in the traditional camp who have little or no appreciation for the word *contemporary*, and the same is true for some in the contemporary camp. The fact is, however, that words have different meanings. In this instance, the word *tradition* not only means fixed, standard, routine, ritual, done in accordance with custom, but also means classic, long established, time-honored, having stood the test of time.

On the other hand, the word *contemporary* is defined as "existing or occurring at the same period of time" (Webster). In other words, to be contemporary is to belong to the present—to be with the times.

These definitions call for pause and reflection. There is value in both traditional and contemporary. God is both the ancient of days, the God of the ages past (Psalm 90), as well as the God of the now, today, "our present help in time of trouble" (Psalm 46). He is the God of both Testaments (Old and New), and is older than time: "Lord, You have been our dwelling place in all generations. Before the mountains were brought forth, or ever You had formed the earth and the world, even from everlasting to everlasting, You are God" (Psalm 90:1, 2). Therefore, to worship in a balanced way is to have some appreciation both for what God is doing in the present as well as for what He has done in the past. Doing so involves valuing music and worship forms of different types and from different eras. God has been inspiring new music and art forms throughout time.

We naturally apply this principle in our secular affairs. We relish modern technology as well as antiques. The owner of a modern vehicle with all the bells and whistles will also take a great amount of pride in owning a Model T Ford. People spend years and lots of money restoring old vehicles, and then devote many hours showing them off at car shows. We value antiques because of what they symbolize: the glory days of the past, ingenuity, creativity, history, the classic and the timeless.

In a similar way, Christians should value what God is doing in the present as well as in the past when it comes to music and worship. God is doing a new thing (Isaiah 42:9) and invites us to create new wineskins to contain the new wine of the Spirit (Matthew 9:17), but His "ancient words are ever true." For some Christians, the choice between that which merely belongs to the present and that which has stood the test of time is usually very simple, except, it seems, when it comes to worship. Some in the traditional camp have no appreciation for things contemporary, and some in the contemporary camp find traditional worship anathema. Thankfully, the objective here is not to get us to choose between the two, but rather, to develop a healthy appreciation for both. Some of the music of the Reformation and many of the hymns penned by writers such as Isaac Watts, John and Charles Wesley, and others, have stood the test of time and are still sung centuries later. Watts' "O God, Our Help in Ages Past" and Luther's "A Mighty Fortress Is Our God" made the order of service at Washington's National Cathedral in the wake of September 11, 2001. No doubt its organizers thought much about the diversity of the audience and how some of these elements would be received. But in times of crisis (personal and national) we naturally turn to the time-tested expressions of faith and confidence in the God who never changes. That's why some of these classic hymns have not gone away. They remain because the Church is rooted in the great doctrines and traditions of "the faith once delivered."

TRADITIONAL VERSUS TRADITIONALISM

Furthermore, there's a difference between tradition and traditionalism. According to Jaroslav Pelikan, "Tradition is the living faith of the dead, traditionalism is the dead faith of the living." The Bible isn't anti-tradition; tradition is not the enemy. There are many great traditions we must hold onto (note 1 Corinthians 11:2, Galatians 1:14; and 2 Thessalonians 2:15 quoted at the beginning of this chapter). Rather, what the Bible is against is traditionalism—dead faith, tradition gone wrong, worship that has no heart in it.

It's been pointed out that the rise of contemporary worship in the mid-twentieth century was in reaction to the formalism that had taken root in the church in the decades prior, prompting a younger generation to embrace the informal when it comes to church and worship. But a grave mistake was made in thinking that the antidote to such formalism is to be informal. The antidote to formalism isn't informality. Rather, it is heart, according to Kevin Swanson. Be it traditional or contemporary, if the heart is not fully engaged, it is useless worship. So let us exercise great care in distinguishing between tradition and traditionalism. Tradition only becomes a problem when it is institutionalized and made into traditionalism. At that point it becomes dead faith and no longer pleases God.

WHEAT AND CHAFF

It is said elsewhere in this book, but it deserves repetition: "Worship is universal in its appeal and practice, but not all worship is acceptable to God." We usually say this in deference to pagan or known false worship, but the distinction between acceptable and non-acceptable worship must also be made within the framework of Christianity itself. When it comes to music and worship styles, we must differentiate between acceptable and unaccept-able—separate the wheat from the chaff. Not every hymn or worship chorus is worth singing. There are traditional hymns that have stood the test of time and there are those that have not. The same is true on the contemporary side of this equation. There are contemporary hymns and worship choruses that have come and gone with the wind and there are those that are here to say. Whether traditional or contemporary, those that remain do so because they are rich in biblical and theological content, and are beautiful in their expres-sion of the story of redemption. "A Mighty Fortress," "And Can it Be," and "When I Survey" are good examples of such classic hymns. Contemporary worship songs also come to mind: "Majesty," "Shout to the Lord," "How Deep the Father's Love for Us," "Before the Throne of God I Stand," "Mighty to Save," and "In Christ Alone." Because of their rich content, these songs will not soon go away, and will be sung by future generations of the church.

Furthermore, many of the traditional hymns are being set to newer tunes to accommodate a younger generation that doesn't relate to the tunes and styles of former eras—God be praised! And we should heed research findings that younger generations (Gen-Xers in particular) are returning to more traditional worship styles. When we stand around the throne in the presence of the Lamb, our worship will not likely be one style. We will join with the redeemed of all ages—including King David, first century believ-ers, the reformers, and many others in between—in ceaseless praise. So let's start now by breaking out of our mold and abandoning our stereotypes. Let's not judge a hymnbook by its cover, nor choose songs merely for their beat or rhythm. Let's select songs on the basis of substance and content, which requires separating wheat from chaff.

WORSHIP'S GUIDING PRINCIPLES

An entire chapter in this book is devoted to what is called Worship's Guiding Principles—biblical guidelines intended to regulate our relationships within the body of Christ. These principles can easily be applied to worship. A summary of them is therefore offered here as an additional consideration in finding balance in this aspect of worship.

Paul admonishes the Church in Rome about what has been called "the principle of preference," as noted in Romans 12:10: "Be kindly affectionate to one another with brotherly love, in honor giving preference to one another." Putting the needs of others above our own is so important in Paul's mind that it remains the prevailing thought through Romans 14 and even in the early verses of chapter 15. In this section of Romans, Paul has much to say about the weaker and the stronger Christian (every disagreement within the body of Christ involves a weaker and a stronger believer), emphasizing that the stronger has a responsibility to protect the spiritual well-being of the weaker. In fact, this is Romans 14 in a nutshell: We should commit ourselves to never knowingly offend a brother or sister for whom Christ died: "I know and am convinced by the Lord Jesus that there is nothing unclean of itself; but to him who considers anything to be unclean, to him it is unclean. Yet if your brother is grieved because of your food, you are no longer walking in love. Do not destroy with your food the one for whom Christ died" (vv. 14, 15). Paul goes on to explain that the living out of this law requires giving up our right to the exercise of our Christian liberty if doing so will cause someone to stumble. Our commitment to giving preference to others instead of looking out for our own interests, our willingness to put the needs of others above our own, will calm many a worship war. The tendency to exercise our personal freedoms without regard for how our actions affect others is a major cause of conflict in Christ's body, and this plays out all too frequently in the area of worship. Worship is not a right to be exercised or an entitlement to be claimed regardless of what others may think. Worship is the expression of love for God, and we cannot love God at the expense of loving and caring for others. So take a moment to read Romans 12–15 and carefully consider the essence of Paul's admonition. Then apply these principles to worship. This will involve prayer, small group discussions, and the input and involvement of local leadership. May this stir us to build bridges across the worship divide, to tear down walls, and to stand together in the worship of the One through whose sacrifice on the cross we've been made *one*.

GENERATIONAL BLESSING

Some who have paid particular attention to the worship landscape have noted that much of the worship divide within the body of Christ in our day results from the failure of one generation of the church to intentionally bless the other. The worship evolution in the American church happened alongside an evolution within the broader culture as our nation "came of age" in the sixties and seventies. A younger generation of Americans had lost faith in both government and church. They were unsettled by the prevailing attitude about race, took exception to the Vietnam War, and questioned the trustworthiness of the government. But their greatest disappointment was over the Church's failure to shine the light of the gospel on these dark issues. So they walked away and formed a movement marked by the way they dressed, the music they played and sang, and the places where they huddled, such as San Francisco, California and Woodstock, Virginia. They were called hippies, and Paul Simon's song "Bridge Over Troubled Water" seemed to precisely reflect the passion of their movement.

But not finding the bridge they were looking for, the hippies eventually returned to church, and how the church reacted to the returning prodigals is a sad tale. Perhaps the church never expected its prodigals to come home. But they did, and they brought their dress code, hairstyle, and music with them, which caused no little discomfort.

But God wastes no opportunity. This tension gave rise to what came to be known as the Jesus Movement, out of which came a new brand of churches populated by this younger generation and marked by non-traditional worship. Alongside this movement came another, the seeker sensitive movement, which considers worship and ministry to be all about making the unchurched (the seeker) feel comfortable and at home in the pew.

This has affected various segments of the church in different ways, and has grown into various sub-movements in the decades since the sixties. But there is general agreement that it is a significant contributor to the worship divide, and many now see a generational issue at the heart of it. Malachi tells us that Messiah's agenda is to turn the hearts of children to their fathers and the hearts of fathers to their children—lest He strike the earth with a curse (4:6). What if in the sixties and seventies a younger generation of the church had demonstrated a different attitude toward the faith of their fathers, and what if an older generation had embraced the new way of the younger upon their return?

In her series on evangelism, Rebecca Manley Pippert tells the true story of a hippie who wandered into the worship service of a large and prestigious traditional style church. Unable to find a seat anywhere in the packed sanctuary, he innocently sat down on the floor in the center aisle in front of the platform. This obviously went against the congregation's culture and worship etiquette, and caused no little distraction as many watched in rapt attention to see what would happen. And sure enough, the first elder, a stately dressed old gentleman, arose, and with the aid of his cane, slowly made his way down the aisle. It was presumed that he would show the young man to a seat, perhaps give him his own. But to everyone's delightful surprise, the old man lowered himself to the floor and sat beside the young man for the remainder of the service. Not only did his willingness to move beyond his comfort zone—to reach out to someone from a younger generation and different style—greatly impact the young man, it changed the disposition of the congregation in a significant way.

BLENDED WORSHIP

Finally, the type of worship encouraged in this chapter is blended worship, that which combines old and new, traditional and contemporary. The book *Planning Blended Worship: The Creative Mixture of Old and New*, by the late Robert Webber, is highly recommended as a resource for planning this type of worship. Webber is only one source; explore others.

AN IMPORTANT QUESTION

Is it ever appropriate for a local church to choose between the two, to primarily (perhaps exclusively) be traditional or contemporary? All things considered, the answer is yes. There are newer churches whose mission and vision target a younger, non-traditional segment of the surrounding culture. There are also older traditional churches that have made a complete shift to the contemporary style to match the changes that have occurred in and around them. The key is that these churches were either raised up on a particular model with no need to choose between the two, or transitioned from one to another in a way that didn't ostracize or cause division.

A good example of the latter is the congregation pastored by nationally known Bible teacher, David Jeremiah, near San Diego, California. Formerly a traditional pipe organ style church known as Scott Memorial Baptist Church, it has completely shifted to contemporary praise-style worship under the name Shadow Mountain Community Church. The name change alone indicates a shift in ministry paradigm and, under Jeremiah's skillful leadership, it has maintained its harmony and growth.

Such success is uncommon; this type of transition is usually more painful. However, the key is acting with concern for the entire body, realizing that none of us has a monopoly on "the right style." There are contemporary churches that are not growing, and there are traditional churches that are expanding their campuses to accommodate growth, and vice versa. It all depends on the standard we set for our congregation. And there are times when it is appropriate to forge a worship path that reflects a particular style.

IN SUMMARY

The comments in this chapter are not offered as a comprehensive treatment of the subject at hand; this only scratches the surface. However, it is hoped that the preceding paragraphs will inspire further study, conversation, and prayer, to the end that the body of Christ will experience less conflict and greater harmony in the area of worship.

REVIEW QUESTIONS

1. What is the significance of the impact of the diversity in the body of Christ on worship?

2. What are *manner* and *mode* in the context of worship?

3. What does the word *traditional* mean?

4. What does the word *contemporary* mean?

5. What is the difference between *tradition* and *traditionalism*?

6. What is *blended worship*?

APPLICATION QUESTIONS

1. Why is it important that worship be rooted in tradition?

2. Why is it important that worship "belong to the present"?

3. In what ways is your congregation diverse?

4. It has been observed that humans were created with the "need" to worship. Consider the diversity in your congregation. How does diversity impact how this need is met? (For example, do children show admiration in the same way that adults do? What about different personality types? Different cultures?)

5. How does Paul define *spiritual strength* and *spiritual weakness*, according to Romans 14?

6. What are 3 ways in which you can put the needs of others above your own in the area of corporate worship?

Endnotes

Scripture quotations were taken from the *New King James Version*.

1. Jaroslav Pelikan, *The Vindication of Tradition* (Yale University Press, reprint edition, 1986), 65.
2. John R. W. Stott, quoted by J. Oswald Sanders in "Intimacy Is Nourished by Worship" (http://www.cslewis-institute.org/webfm_send/556). Web accessed 9-9-15.
3. Quoted by Desmond Ford in "The Gulf War and Bible Prophecy – 1" (https://www.goodnewsunlimited.com/gulf-war-bible-prophecy-1-desmond-ford/). Web accessed 9-9-15.

CHAPTER 11

FINDING BALANCE (PART 2)

WORD AND WORSHIP

That epic encounter between God and the nation of Israel at Mount Sinai was as much about the revelation of the pattern for the tabernacle as it was about the giving of the law. The law points to the Word of God; the tabernacle points to our worship of God. Therefore, living out the true meaning of Sinai requires balancing Word and worship.

After reading this chapter, you will be able to

- define *legalism*;
- define *fanaticism*;
- describe the relationship between the giving of the law, Shavuot, and the significance of Pentecost to Christians;
- describe the relationship between ministry, worship, and the Holy Spirit;

- describe the relationship between worship and understanding the Word of God.

And we have such trust through Christ toward God. Not that we are sufficient of ourselves to think of anything as being from ourselves, but our sufficiency is from God, who also made us sufficient as ministers of the new covenant, not of the letter but of the Spirit; for the letter kills, but the Spirit gives life (2 Corinthians 3:4–6).

"But the hour is coming, and now is, when the true worshipers will worship the Father in spirit and truth; for the Father is seeking such to worship Him. God is Spirit, and those who worship Him must worship in spirit and truth" (John 4:23, 24).

It may well be that many believers have spent most of their spiritual journey camped at Sinai without grasping the whole of what God revealed there.

In Scripture Sinai corresponds with Pentecost, and, as J. Oswald Sanders masterfully illustrates, Pentecost is forever connected with the coming of the Holy Spirit.[1]

The ongoing debate between Christianity and secular culture over the place of the Ten Commandments in the public square is evidence of the intrinsic value of "the Big Ten" and their impact on people's conscience. That's why they're still on people's minds, religious and secular, despite changes in society. What God said at Sinai wasn't just instructive for Israel; it has spiritual import for all people throughout history. The Ten Commandments were not only given to God's chosen people as its charter, they are intended to define sin and morality for all humanity, in every generation. Paul affirmed this when he wrote, "What shall we say, then? Is the law sinful? Certainly not! Nevertheless, I would not have known what sin was had it not been for the law" (Romans 7:7, NIV).

But our emphasis on the commandments must be held in balance with equal emphasis on the other half of what God revealed at Sinai. What else did God reveal there? God also revealed the pattern for the construction of the tabernacle. Read the book of Exodus and note how many chapters are devoted to the details concerning the tabernacle. And what was the purpose of the tabernacle? The tabernacle was about worship, the place where the priests ordered things pertaining to the various sacrifices and offerings. The detailed instructions recorded by Moses not only provided the blueprint for the building but a pattern for the worship that the building was to facilitate. So the law points to the Word of God and our walk of obedience to it, while the tabernacle points to the worship of God and our walk before Him in praise and devotion. Sinai is not about the giving of the Ten Commandments with side commentary about the tabernacle. Sinai was as much about the revelation of the pattern for the tabernacle as it was about the giving of the Ten Commandments. Therefore, Sinai is a call to balance the Word of God (law) with the worship of God (Spirit). Not only are we a people of the Word, we are also a people of worship, a people of the law, and a people of the Spirit.

Balancing Word and worship is important because (according to the old axiom), "Word without worship tends toward legalism, and worship without the Word leads to fanaticism." Legalism is the unhealthy approach to Scripture whereby, according to popular author Max Lucado, we make our convictions other people's obligations. And fanaticism, according to Webster, is "excessive enthusiasm, intense uncritical devotion." So both legalism and fanaticism are to be avoided, and the key is balance.

Thus, in that epic encounter at Sinai, God, in His infinite wisdom, not only gave Israel the details of the law, but also a pattern for the tabernacle. And the purpose of the tabernacle is worship.

Furthermore, we derive from Scripture that the giving of the law at Sinai corresponds with the coming of the Spirit at Pentecost. The English word Pentecost is a transliteration of the Greek word pentekostos, which means "fifty." It refers to the Hebrew Festival of Weeks, known in the Hebrew as Shavuot, an expression derived from Leviticus 23:16, which instructs the Israelites to count seven weeks or "fifty days" from the end of Passover to the beginning of the next holy day—Pentecost. Shavuot was the second great feast in Israel's yearly cycle of festivals or holy days. Originally a harvest festival (Exodus 23:16), it eventually evolved into the commemoration of the giving of the law at Sinai. Looking back from the vantage point of the New Testament, we see that this pointed to the coming of the Spirit in Acts 2, which, as it turned out, happened during the celebration of Shavuot or Pentecost, exactly seven weeks (fifty days) after the resurrection of Jesus, our Passover. Looking back, we also see that this harvest festival foreshadowed the first harvest of souls reaped in the ministry of the early church when three thousand were converted through Peter's preaching.

Still, the question remains: Why does Pentecost matter to New Testament Christians? J. Oswald Sanders writes, "Pentecost is second only to Calvary in importance to the Christian, for Pentecost is the complement of Calvary....for all Christian experience revolves around the twin centres of Calvary and Pentecost. Calvary opened the fountain from which all of the blessings of Pentecost flowed. Pentecost made available to men all that Calvary made possible."[2] Sanders' answer is insightful. He writes in a later paragraph, "Had Pentecost been omitted from the Divine counsels, it would have been like perfecting a costly machine, and then failing to supply it with the necessary motive power."[3] So to answer the question, Pentecost matters to Christians because it symbolizes the empowerment of believers by the Spirit of God. Jesus' instruction to His disciples to not leave the upper room until they were endued with power is also instructive for us. Ministry must be done in the power of the Spirit, not in the energy of the flesh. Effective ministry must be preceded by time spent in the "upper room" seeking the Spirit's power.

Sinai is therefore a reminder that worship is not an invention of New Testament Christians; it has always been God's design for His people. God created us for the purpose of worship. It is a central theme of Scripture, from the altars of Genesis, to the songs of Revelation. Therefore, experiencing the fullness of God's presence and power as individuals and as a church is directly related to our capacity to honor God with biblical worship. And biblical worship is balanced worship. The two items on the balance scale in this instance are Word and worship—law and Spirit. It's been rightly pointed out that it is the depth of our ministry in the Word of God that determines the quality and depth of our worship. And we might add that it is the depth and quality of our worship that determines the effect of the Word in our lives. We need the Bible to instruct us, and we need the Spirit of God to empower us to walk in obedience to the Bible's instructions. As noted earlier, the notion that "I'm a commandment-keeping Christian who majors on the Word, but

I'm not much into worship" is woefully misguided. Similarly, the notion that says, "I'm here to worship; I'm not much into the Word" is misguided as well. To be a student of the Word is to be a worshipper. To be a worshipper is to be a student of the Word. So by the grace of God, let's hold these two essentials in good balance. Let us traverse both the upper slopes of Sinai as well as the upper room, the richness and beauty of God's Word and the power of the Holy Spirit. The result will be balanced worship. Remember that "the letter kills, but the Spirit gives life" (2 Corinthians 3:6).

> "It is the depth of our worship service ministry in the Word that will determine the height of our worship. If we are superficial in the ministry of the Word of God, then our worship of God will be equally superficial."
> — Dr. Steven Lawson

WORD AND SPIRIT

All word and no spirit, we dry up; all Spirit and no Word, we blow up; both Word and Spirit, we grow up.[4]
— David Watson

REVIEW QUESTIONS

1. What is *legalism*?

2. What is *fanaticism*?

3. What is the relationship between the giving of the law, Shavuot, and the significance of Pentecost to Christians?

4. What is the relationship between ministry, worship, and the Holy Spirit?

5. What is the relationship between worship and understanding the Word of God?

APPLICATION QUESTIONS

1. Although we strive for balance, perfect balance is difficult to attain. Even if the difference is slight, are you more comfortable studying the Word or engaging in active, intentional worship? Why do you think you are more drawn to this?

2. Worship should be a natural outflow of studying the Word. Why might it be possible for us to study the Word and *not* respond in worship?

3. Worship is a response to a revelation of who God has revealed Himself to be. How might worship without study lead to fanaticism?

4. How does the Holy Spirit empower your worship?

5. "To be a worshipper is to be a student of the Word." What does it mean to be a student of the Word? What is one step you can take to become a better student of the Word?

Endnotes

Scripture quotations were taken from the *New King James Version*, unless otherwise noted.

1. J. Oswald Sanders, *The Holy Spirit and His Gifts* (Grand Rapids: Lamplighter Books, 1940), 48–54.
2. Ibid., 48.
3. Ibid.
4. David Watson, *I Believe in the Church*, as quoted by Richard A. Kauffman in "The Word of God," *Christianity Today* (October 22, 2001), http://www.christianitytoday.com/ct/2001/october22/23.40.html. Web accessed 10-15-15.

CHAPTER 12

WORSHIP'S GUIDING PRINCIPLES

Scripture allows much latitude in style, culture, and personality when it comes to worship, but it doesn't leave us without overarching principles that can guide us in our search for unity and balance.

After reading this chapter, you will be able to

- define and critique the *Regulative Principle of Worship* (RPW);
- define *asceticism*;
- define *Christian liberty*;
- list three guiding principles for worship practices.

Therefore let us pursue the things which make for peace and the things by which one may edify another. Do not destroy the work of God for the sake of food. All things indeed are pure, but it is evil for the man who eats with offense. It is good neither to eat meat nor drink wine nor do anything by which your brother stumbles or is offended or is made weak (Romans 14:19–21).

"...the regulative principle as applied to public worship frees the church from acts of impropriety and idiocy...."[1]

C hristians in every age must discern the difference between that which God requires or prescribes for His people in Scripture and that which is merely a matter of personal or cultural preference. This became an important principle in the life of the first century church. A good example is the question of whether or not it was appropriate for Christians to eat meats sacrificed to idols. Apparently, after offering their sacrifices, the idol worshippers would sell the meat in the marketplace. Those from that background now converted to Christ were particularly sensitive to this and went to great lengths, not only to avoid eating such meats but to ensure that their fellow brethren didn't either. Paul therefore addressed this by pointing out that the meat itself was not inherently bad. Reformed theologians later coined the term "matters of ethical indifference" to describe this principle. In our day, this would translate to questions about watching television, going to the movies, wearing makeup, dancing, etc.

Needless to say, such matters are not specifically addressed in Scripture. Some of them didn't exist when the Bible was being inspired. But what about similar discrepancies regarding worship? Should we sing only classical hymns or should praise choruses be allowed? What about drums? Since the Bible doesn't specifically address these, how do we deal with them in a way that honors the Lord and makes for Christian unity?

It was this question, the need to address issues of corporate and public worship in a biblical and systematic way, which led the reformers to craft what has come to be known as the Regulative Principle of Worship (RPW). It essentially says that the church's corporate worship must be guided by specific directives from Scripture. However, over the centuries, the RPW has become the guide for Puritan and Presbyterian worship. A very rigid form of the RPW stipulated that "what is commanded is required; what is not commanded is forbidden."[2]

If that statement raises a red flag for you, it should. The first half is reasonable, but the second half would prohibit most of what we do in public worship. To be sure, the Bible makes specific statements from which the guiding principle for God-honoring worship may be gleaned. For example:

- The story of Cain and Abel teaches that we must worship God according to His requirements, not our preferences (Genesis 4:3–8).
- We note in Exodus 20:2–6 that the first two of the Ten Commandments are precise about our worship of the one true God, and prohibits the worship of idols.
- God was very specific when instructing Moses about the construction of the tabernacle of worship: "See to it that you make them according to the pattern which was shown you" (Exodus 25:40).
- The making of the golden calf and God's subsequent judgement of the people is a reminder that the human heart is prone to idolatry, that even those brought out of Egypt (a picture of those redeemed from sin) faced the temptation to return to the gods of the past, to substitute the worship of a hand-made image for the worship of the true God, which He detests and judges severely.
- God killed people for offering "strange fire" as acceptable worship. We learn this from the story of Nadab and Abihu in Leviticus 10. In fact, that could be taken a step further. Read the Old Testament; God destroyed whole nations in order to eradicate idolatry. The command to destroy the Canaanite nations is a prime example.
- God rejected Saul's unprescribed offering in 1 Samuel 15, and reminded Saul that "obedience is better than sacrifice."
- Jesus rebuked the Pharisees for placing too great a value on "the tradition of the elders" in Matthew 15:14.
- Paul spends much time in his first letter to the Corinthians addressing the issue of the public manifestation of the gift of tongues, and lays down the ground rules (see 1 Corinthians 14:26–33).
- Finally, Paul had this special counsel for the church in Colosse: "These things indeed have an appearance of wisdom in self-imposed religion, false humility, and neglect of the body, but are of no value against the

indulgence of the flesh" (Colossians 2:23). The concern here is ascet-icism, the attempt to achieve righteousness by self-denial and self-neglect, which Paul calls "self-imposed religion."

The New Testament isn't silent regarding things acceptable and not acceptable in Christian worship, as these references show. But though help-ful, they don't address all of the complex issues involved in modern worship. Thankfully, some reformed theologians concede that such a view of the RPW is extreme, that there are many things we do in worship that are entirely appropriate though not expressly commanded in Scripture, that the passion of the RPW isn't about contemporary vs. traditional forms of worship, how many verses of a hymn should be sung, or the length of a prayer; but rather, that "all things be done decently and in order" (1 Corinthians 14:40). And it is in the spirit of this admonition to do all things decently and in order that the following guiding principles of worship are drawn from the writings of Paul. They fall under the category of Christian liberty—the believer's freedom to act on the basis of conscience where there is no express command or instruc-tion in Scripture.

First, we note Paul's admonition to the Galatian congregation to not bind the conscience regarding matters on which the Bible is silent: "Stand fast therefore in the liberty by which Christ has made us free, and do not be entangled again with a yoke of bondage" (Galatians 5:1). Reading the next five verses reveals that what Paul had in mind in this case was circumcision, which he regarded as a matter of indifference—matters on which Scripture allows a great degree of latitude. Interestingly, Paul treated this matter according to the particular circumstance. In the case of Titus (Galatians 2:3) he opposed circumcision, while in the case of Timothy (Acts 16:3) he almost insisted upon it. The principle here is honoring Christian liberty—to not put a burden (yoke) on ourselves, and especially on other believers, in matters on which the Bible places no such burden. Relating to worship, we may feel strongly about an issue, but if it isn't a matter of clear biblical command or instruction, we must not treat it as if it is. In so doing we allow latitude, avoid division, and our personal conviction does not become someone else's obligation.

Second, Paul admonishes the Corinthians to set boundaries for the exercise of their Christian liberty: "All things are lawful for me, but all things are not helpful. All things are lawful for me, but I will not be brought under the power of any" (1 Corinthians 6:12). In other words, our rights or freedoms as believers should always be exercised with this question in mind: Is this mutually beneficial and edifying? If the answer is "no," then exercising such freedom places personal gratification above spiritual concern and edification, which does not glorify God. The context for this admonition is the use of our bodies, the need to avoid excess, being careful to walk clear of immorality (read through the end of the chapter). Applied to worship, the guiding principle is to always ask the question of spiritual benefit and edification. Is the exercise of this freedom honoring Christ, or simply feeding my lower nature?

Third, Paul takes the previous principle a step further in 1 Corinthians 8. Read the entire chapter, giving close attention to verses 9–13:

> But beware lest somehow this liberty of yours become a stumbling block to those who are weak. For if anyone sees you who have knowledge eating in an idol's temple, will not the conscience of him who is weak be emboldened to eat those things offered to idols? And because of your knowledge shall the weak brother perish, for whom Christ died? But when you thus sin against the brethren, and wound their weak conscience, you sin against Christ. Therefore, if food makes my brother stumble, I will never again eat meat, lest I make my brother stumble.

Here Paul deals again with the subject of meats sacrificed to idols. Whereas he previously told the Corinthians that such meat isn't inherently bad, he now places the freedom to eat such meat under a much higher principle—the effect our actions have on other believers. Not only should we be concerned about how the exercise of our freedom affects us spiritually, we must be equally concerned about its impact on other members of Christ's body. Even in matters of indifference, we must never be indifferent to the need to do all things to the glory of God, to do all things in decency and in order, to make sure that our actions aren't causing others to stumble.

The application of this principle to worship is rather clear. Many a "worship war" would cease and Christ's body would know much greater harmony if worshipers would apply this principle in the exercise of their freedom. Some of the tension in the contemporary worship scene is the determination of some believers to exercise their "worship freedom" in an "in your face" kind of way, not caring for the needs and concerns for the rest of the body. And since the emphasis here is balance, it should be added that the same is true of those on the opposite side of the worship aisle. There are those who are so committed to the traditional style that they do not consider its effect on others in the congregation. This ought not to be. In treating this matter at length in Romans 14, Paul appeals to the "law of love," and reminds the church in Rome to commit to never offend a brother (or sister) for whom Christ died (see vv. 14, 15).

In summary, the guiding principles for worship are 1) to not bind the conscience in matters on which the Bible is silent, 2) to always ask the question of mutual benefit and edification, and 3) to be concerned about how the exercise of my Christian liberty affects others within the body of Christ. Remember the old axiom:

> Methods are many,
> Principles are few;
> Methods may change,
> But Principles never do.

REVIEW QUESTIONS

1. What is the Regulative Principle of Worship, and why should it raise a red flag?

2. What is *asceticism*?

3. What is *Christian liberty*?

4. What are three guiding principles for worship practices?

APPLICATION QUESTIONS

1. Regarding Christian liberty, is there a difference between feeling strongly about an issue (putting a burden on ourselves), and insisting that others should feel strongly about it, too (putting that burden on other believers)? [key word = insist]

2. What are five current "matters" regarding worship in which the Bible is silent/not explicit?

3. How are these issues impacting the unity of your congregation?

4. How might these issues be involved in "causing others to stumble"?

5. How can you demonstrate care for the needs and concerns of the rest of the body regarding worship?

Endnotes

Scripture quotations were taken from the *New King James Version.*

1. Derek W. H. Thomas, "The Regulative Principle of Worship," *Tabletalk* (July 2010), 12.
2. Quoted by R. J. Gore Jr., "Adiaphora in Worship," *Tabletalk* (July 2010), 14.

CHAPTER 13

A LIFESTYLE OF SINGING

Live a life of worship. But never think that is a substitute for singing the songs of worship.

After reading this chapter, you will be able to

- describe what it means that worship is a lifestyle;
- list five activities, besides singing, that can be offered to God as worship;
- compare and contrast living a life of worship with singing the songs of worship;
- explain why singing is a vital part of worship, despite the fact that all activities can be offered as worship.

Whether, then, you eat or drink or whatever you do, do all to the glory of God (1 Corinthians 10:31).

"Songs of worship arise from a life of worship."

— *Tim Hughes*

Worship is a lifestyle. While we might easily agree with this statement at face value, sometimes our language reveals that our vision of worship is far too narrow. We call Sabbath our "day of worship" and our time together on Sabbath mornings a "worship service." Even in these meetings, we often call the singing portion of the service "worship," but the prayer, preaching and other activities something *other* than worship.

The truth is that, for many, *worship* is nothing more than a synonym for *Christian music.*

Yet Scripture reveals that the entirety of our life—not just the songs we sing—should be devoted to God as worship. Two passages immediately come to mind in this regard.

In 1 Corinthians 10, Paul is talking about the issue of meat offered to idols. In Corinth, the people were dividing over whether eating such meat was acceptable for Christians. Paul talks about this specific issue, but then points them to a higher principle. Just as he does in Romans 14, Paul emphasizes the importance of caring more about each other than they care about their food. Convictions about what we eat are important, but should never be used to tear each other down or cause each other to stumble. So it is that Paul summarizes his thoughts in 1 Corinthians 10 with these words:

Whether, then, you eat or drink or whatever you do, do all to the glory of God (v. 31).

Another passage is found in Colossians 3. There Paul is instructing various household members how to do everything that they do "in the name of the Lord Jesus" (v. 17). He finishes the section by saying,

> Whatever you do, do your work heartily, as for the Lord rather than
> for men, knowing that from the Lord you will receive the reward of the
> inheritance. It is the Lord Christ whom you serve (vv. 23, 24).

Taken together, these two passages convey an important reality about our lives. Whatever we do—even the mundane tasks of working, eating, and drinking—is to be done in service to Christ and to the glory of God.

So, what does this have to do with worship?

Perhaps the simplest definition of worship is to *glorify* God. Paul teaches us that whatever we do should be done to the glory of God. So it is that every part of our life should be worship. But how can activities such as working, eating and drinking be worship? How can the daily tasks of the business executive, teacher, housewife, plumber, or software engineer glorify God?

The answer is this. When we engage in our daily activities in order to show love to God and to our neighbor, those activities become worship. Every action of our lives, no matter how seemingly trivial or menial, can be devoted to God as worship.

In reality, our daily activities are always worship. The question is not whether we are worshipping when we work or eat or play or rest. The question is, who are we worshipping? Are we worshipping self, culture, money, or power? Or are we worshipping God?

The call of God throughout Scripture is for us to devote every activity of life, every moment of every day to worshipping God. This doesn't mean that we spend all day praying and reading our Bibles. As vital as these particular activities are, they are hardly all that God has in mind for us. Rather, God created us to live lives full of relationships, responsibility and rest. It is the devotion of every aspect of our lives—relationships, responsibilities and rest—to God that makes it a life of worship.

So worship is a lifestyle.

For some, this realization raises the question, "If everything I do in life can be devoted to God as worship, why do I need to sing?"

Many Christians can't sing well or lack confidence in their singing. For some, the weekly gatherings that call for them to sing in public are uncomfortable. Others enjoy singing, but don't particularly care for the style of music their congregation sings. Still others, regardless of their singing preferences, don't experience a sense of intimacy with God while singing. They find that the same time could be devoted to other activities in which they would feel connected and sense that God was being glorified.

So, why do we sing?

Music features prominently throughout Scripture in the worship of God. When God established the ministry of the temple, a major component of that ministry was musical worship. Teams of professional, skilled worship leaders were selected to lead the people in song as part of offering themselves—not just their animals—to God. These worship leaders were housed in the temple itself and made their living from daily devotion to music ministry (1 Chronicles 9:33, 34). They led the people, raising voices and instruments in praise to God (1 Chronicles 15:16–22), and ushering in the presence of God (2 Chronicles 5:11–14).

Throughout Scripture we see God's people composing and singing songs to God in honor of Him and His gracious acts. Consider a few examples. In Exodus 15, following the crossing of the Red Sea, we find the song of Moses and Miriam. In Judges 5, following a victory over the Canaanites, we read the song of Deborah and Barak. David's life was full of song as he wrote dozens of psalms expressing the full breadth of human emotion, glorifying God through pain, repentance, joy, and praise. In the New Testament we find Paul and Silas singing praise to God at midnight in a Philippian jail (Acts 16:25). And the most extended worship scene in all of Scripture—Revelation 4–5— unveils the glory of worship in which the heavenly host joins all of creation in lifting up new songs of praise to God.

Throughout Scripture, the people of God are invited to follow these gifted musicians in song. Psalms 66 and 150 are just two examples of an entire group of psalms that called God's covenant people—and indeed, all creation— to worship Him in song:

> Shout joyfully to God, all the earth;
> Sing glory to His name;
>> Make His praise glorious.
> Say to God, "How awesome are Your works!
>> Because of the greatness of Your power Your enemies will give
>>> feigned obedience to You.
> "All the earth will worship You,
>> And will sing praises to You;
>> They will sing praises to Your name" (Psalm 66:1–4).

> Praise the Lord!
>> Praise God in His sanctuary;
>> Praise Him in His mighty expanse.
> Praise Him for His mighty deeds;
>> Praise Him according to His excellent greatness.

> Praise Him with trumpet sound;
>> Praise Him with harp and lyre.
> Praise Him with timbrel and dancing;
>> Praise Him with stringed instruments and pipe;
> Praise Him with loud cymbals;
>> Praise Him with resounding cymbals.
> Let everything that has breath praise the Lord.
>> Praise the Lord! (Psalm 150).

The call is repeated in the New Testament in twin passages from Paul's letters:

> And do not get drunk with wine, for that is dissipation, but be filled with the Spirit, speaking to one another in psalms and hymns and spiritual songs, singing and making melody with your heart to the Lord; always giving thanks for all things in the name of our Lord Jesus Christ to God, even the Father (Ephesians 5:18–20).

> Let the word of Christ richly dwell within you, with all wisdom teaching and admonishing one another with psalms and hymns and spiritual songs, singing with thankfulness in your hearts to God (Colossians 3:16).

When we answer this call to worship God in song, we join the heavenly chorus of Revelation 4–5, giving honor to God and edifying each other. Worship is a lifestyle, but the act of singing and offering musical worship is a necessary and rich expression of worship for individual Christians and the body of Christ corporately. In his daily devotional, *Your Father Loves You*, J. I. Packer explains it this way:

> This then is worship in its largest sense: petition as well as praise, preaching as well as prayer, hearing as well as speaking, actions as well as words, obeying as well as offering, loving people as well as loving God. However, the primary acts of worship are those which focus on God directly—and we must not imagine that work for God in the world is a substitute for direct fellowship with him in praise and prayer and devotion.[1]

And we should expect it to be this way. We are in a relationship of love with God. In any loving relationship there is the need for time spent and energy devoted to simply adoring the object of our affection. Consider my role as a husband.

I can work all day at my job to provide for my wife's physical needs. I can do all the projects on the "honey-do" list around the house to contribute to her comfort. I can be a wonderful father to our children. I can speak with her about work and church and recreation and entertainment and social issues and any number of topics. But there is no substitute for showering her with praise, affirming her worth, adoring her person and finding my greatest joy in simply being intimate with her.

So it is in our relationship with God.

Every element of our life should be offered as worship to God, but no investment in other relationships, responsibilities or rest can substitute for simply coming before God and adoring His person, praising His work, and joining with the saints in lifting Him up in musical praise.

So live a life of worship. But never think that is a substitute for singing the songs of worship. Rather, let the songs of worship become the soundtrack to a life lived in constant devotion to the God who is worthy of all our praise.

REVIEW QUESTIONS

1. What does it mean to say that "worship is a lifestyle"?

2. What are five activities, besides singing, that can be offered to God as worship?

3. Compare and contrast living a life of worship with singing the songs of worship.

4. Why is singing a vital part of worship, despite the fact that all activities can be offered as worship?

APPLICATION QUESTIONS

1. How are you glorifying God (showing love to Him and neighbor) when you eat? Work? Rest? Play?

2. Consider the activities listed above. How can you bring more glory to Him in each of these activities?

3. Do you feel uncomfortable singing? Do you care for the style of music that your congregation sings? Do you experience a sense of intimacy with God when singing? If you answered 'no' to any of these questions, how does this chapter impact your approach to worship through singing?

Endnotes

Scripture quotations were taken from the *New American Standard Bible*.

1. James I. Packer, *Your Father Loves You* (Harold Shaw Publishers, 1986), 15.

CHAPTER 14

MEANING WHAT WE SING

Our singing should always be authentic and true. However, lofty words can call us to higher heights and deeper depths of devotion to God than what we currently feel or have previously experienced.

After reading this chapter, you will be able to

- compare and contrast distraction and disconnection when it comes to insincere singing;
- list five common issues that tend to distract us from wholehearted worship;
- describe how singing songs of dedication can serve to convict, inspire, and strengthen;
- discuss ways in which we might sing certain affirmations as requests or recommitments.

Let the word of Christ richly dwell within you, with all wisdom teaching and admonishing one another with psalms and hymns and spiritual songs, singing with thankfulness in your hearts to God (Colossians 3:16).

"We may be truly said to worship God, though we want perfection; but we cannot be said to worship Him if we want sincerity. A statue upon a tomb, with eyes and hands lifted up, offers as good and true a service; it wants only a voice, the gestures and postures are the same—nay, the service is better; it is not a mockery, it represents all that it can be framed to. But to worship without our spirits is presenting God with a picture, an echo, voice, and nothing else—a compliment, a mere lie."

— Stephen Charnock

"When I worship, I would rather my heart be without words than my words be without heart."

— Lamar Boschman

❝ ...this people draw near with their words
    And honor Me with their lip service,
    But they remove their hearts far from Me,
    And their reverence for Me consists of tradition learned by rote"
(Isaiah 29:13).

Passages like this are familiar to us. They stand as a warning against insincere and empty worship. They remind us that the mouth and heart are not always connected. It is possible to sing and pray and say all the right words, while inwardly we are distracted, distant, even disconnected.

The temptation exists for all of us who have grown familiar with the songs we sing. We get to the point where we don't need the words in the hymnal or on the projector screen. In fact, we don't even need them in our hearts.

The words of the songs become tradition learned through weekly repetition. We internalize them through rote memorization. And if we are not careful, we can sing them while our minds are on the chore list at home, the

worries of the work week, the football game, the kids' recital or the unre-
solved conflict with the sister in the next row.

Beyond this level of distraction, there is a deeper risk of disconnect from
the songs we sing. Like the people Isaiah prophesied to, there is the risk of
singing all the right songs while living a life that is in direct contradiction to
those songs. Many of our songs contain confessions of love for God, devotion
to Christ, willingness to sacrifice ourselves, commitments to be united and
faithful to one another. When the reality is that our love has grown cold, our
devotion has waned, selfishness has won the day and we are divided from
one another, these songs can become nothing more than a charade.

We can become like some of the religious leaders of Jesus' day who
worked so hard to clean up the outside, while inwardly they were dead and
dirty (Matthew 23). We can become experts at hypocrisy, putting on a show
for those around us, when we know that the songs we sing and the prayers
we pray do not represent the truth of what is in our hearts and lives. Ultimately, we can begin singing songs for one another and ourselves, rather
than for the God to whom they are addressed.

But God desires sincere worship.

God desires, not only lip service, but hearts and lives that are devoted to
Him. God desires for us to worship Him in every aspect of our lives, so that
our songs are simply an overflow of a life lived for Him. God desires that
when we sing to Him our minds are set on Him and not distracted by the
cares of life. God desires that our relationships with others be kept in good
health so that they are not a distraction from our relationship with Him.
While we might know the words of the songs by rote memorization, God
desires that we sing them new and fresh and genuinely each and every time
we offer them to Him.

We could stop at this point and have said something worth saying about
sincerity in worship. However, there is another issue to explore in trying to
be authentic in our singing. On one hand, we should sing in a focused way,
keeping our minds set on the object of our worship. We should sing honestly,
thinking carefully about what we are saying, and only saying those things
that we mean from our hearts.

On the other hand, singing is a unique opportunity for confession,
aspiration, and transformation. Sometimes, through singing we encourage
and recommit ourselves to confessions that are not true of us at present, but

represent a prayer of what we hope to become. Two well-known songs come to mind in this regard.

I think first of the classic hymn by Judson W. Van De Venter:

> All to Jesus I surrender;
> All to Him I freely give;
> I will ever love and trust Him,
> In His presence daily live.
> I surrender all,
> I surrender all;
> All to Thee, my blessed Savior,
> I surrender all.

We have all sung this song, but how often have we reflected on the absolute and exclusive nature of its words? How many of us can honestly claim to have surrendered and freely given everything we are and everything we have to God? While this is the call to anyone who would be Christ's disciple, few of us could sincerely claim that we have learned to fully answer that call. Living in God's presence daily is an aspiration, but not a reality, for most of us who sing this song. We desire to surrender all but, day after day, year after year, God reveals to us territories of our heart and areas of our lives that have been withheld. Total surrender to God is an ongoing journey of the Christian life, not a past destination to look back on.

So, should we continue singing such a song, if we cannot sing it *honestly*? Here is where balance is needed. Some songs that we sing express a reality of our current relationship with God. Others, like "I Surrender All," express an aspiration, a hope, a desire. More than this, they express a commitment and a confidence that He who began a good work in us will bring it to completion.

To sing "I Surrender All" is not to hypocritically profess something that is not true. Rather, it is the cry of a surrendered heart to surrender all that remains unconquered by Christ. It is a confession and a prayer. When we sing it in this way, we can sing it sincerely and truly, with our hearts and lips aligned.

The second song that comes to mind in this regard is the modern hymn "You Are My King (Amazing Love)." The final line of the chorus reads,

> It's my joy to honor You
> In all I do, I honor You.[1]

Once more we're faced with a convicting question, "Is it true that I honor God in everything I do?" If we're honest, we'll note a variety of things in our lives that do not honor God. We are all prone to thoughts, words and actions that actually dishonor God. Does this disqualify us from singing "You Are My King (Amazing Love)"?

The answer is not a simple one. In some cases, lyrics like these should serve as a mouth-stopping conviction. At times I've been singing this song and come to this line only to find myself silenced. I have become overwhelmed by the reality of sin in my life that is keeping me from honoring God. Such moments have called me to confession and repentance. At other times, I've sung the song with a clear conscience before God, offering the words to God as a vow and a recognition that in Christ, the totality of my life can bring honor to God. In many cases, I tend to modify the words of this song to more closely match my current reality. So, I sing wholeheartedly, "It's my joy to honor You/In all I do, I *want to* honor You." This subtle modification changes an affirmation to a prayer.

Many songs with lofty lyrics offer us the opportunity to sing them as confessions, prayers, aspirations, hopes and commitments, rather than declarations of the way things are. God knows the heart and the intent of the words when we sing them. When we put our thoughts on Him and sing the words in sincerity and truth, He hears them in kind.

So, we are called to balance. On one hand, we must never allow our singing to become an empty charade, divorced from the reality of our lives or the object of our attention. God deserves our entire lives and He deserves our thoughts and emotions when we sing to Him. Distraction, distance, and disconnect have no place in our musical worship.

On the other hand, musical worship is an opportunity to refocus the mind, draw closer in intimacy, and bridge the gap between our daily life and our desire for perfect righteousness. Singing to God is a form of prayer in which confession, repentance and aspiration can occur. Through singing we encourage one another and re-commit ourselves to confessions that may not be true of us at present, but represent a prayer of what we hope to become. In return, God responds with transformation as we yield ourselves to the sanctifying work of His Spirit.

So I invite you to mean what you sing, but to sing what you mean. God is listening.

REVIEW QUESTIONS

1. How are distraction and disconnection similar when it comes to insincere singing? How are they different?

2. What are five common issues that tend to distract us from wholehearted worship?

3. How can singing songs of dedication serve to convict, inspire, and strengthen us?

4. How might affirmations be sung as requests or recommitments?

APPLICATION QUESTIONS

1. When are you most likely to disconnect from worship? What steps can you take to prevent or address this?

2. What is most likely to distract you from wholehearted worship? What steps can you take to minimize this distraction?

3. Has a song of dedication ever served to convict, inspire or strengthen you? What was the song? How did it impact you?

4. Give three examples of "mouth-stopping lyrics." How might they be sung as a request or a recommitment?

Endnotes

Scripture quotations were taken from the *New American Standard Bible.*

1. "You Are My King (Amazing Love)" by Billy James Foote. Copyright © 1999 Worshiptogether.com Songs (ASCAP) (adm. at CapitolCMGPublishing.com) All rights reserved. Used by permission.

CHAPTER 15

THE PATTERN OF WORSHIP

The pattern given to Moses by God for the construction of the Old Testament tabernacle reveals a pattern for New Testament worship.

As a result of reading this chapter, you will be able to

- identify God's grand objective in redeeming the nation of Israel out of Egyptian bondage;
- identify what qualifies us to come into God's presence;
- describe the significance of our need for ongoing sanctification;
- identify the goal of the Christian life and the key to realizing this goal;
- describe the effect of Christ's light on worshippers;
- describe how what element of the tabernacle symbolizes the fellowship of prayer;
- identify a pattern of worship that emerges from the ark and the mercy seat;

- list the six components of the pattern of worship observed in the tabernacle.

How lovely is your tabernacle, O Lord of hosts! (Psalm 84:1).

And let them make Me a sanctuary, that I may dwell among them. According to all that I show you, that is, the pattern of the tabernacle and the pattern of all its furnishings, just so you shall make it (Exodus 25:8, 9).

Now when these things had been thus prepared, the priests always went into the first part of the tabernacle, performing the services. But into the second part the high priest went alone once a year, not without blood, which he offered for himself and for the people's sins committed in ignorance; the Holy Spirit indicating this, that the way into the Holiest of All was not yet made manifest while the first tabernacle was still standing. It was symbolic for the present time in which both gifts and sacrifices are offered which cannot make him who performed the service perfect in regard to the conscience—concerned only with foods and drinks, various washings, and fleshly ordinances imposed until the time of reformation (Hebrews 9:6-10).

"The layout of the tabernacle is perhaps the most detailed explanation of salvation in the Old Testament."

— Author Unknown

Sinai was an early and significant stopping point in Israel's journey through the wilderness. In his unforgettable encounter at the burning bush, Moses was assured by God that when he brought the Israelites out of Egypt they would worship Him on that very mountain: "So He said, 'I will certainly be with you. And this shall be a sign to you that I have sent you: When you have brought the people out of Egypt, you shall serve God on this mountain'" (Exodus 3:12). In fact, in trying to convince Pharaoh to let the people go, Moses' strongest argument was that they needed to go three days' journey into the wilderness so they could worship God (see Exodus 5:3). Worship was God's grand objective in redeeming the nation of Israel out of Egyptian bondage.

Now only a short time after leaving Egypt, they arrived at the appointed place—Sinai, "the mountain of God." There the Israelites camped for an extended period of time as God carefully revealed 1) the laws and statutes and 2) the pattern for the construction of the tabernacle. The revelation of the law was to prepare the people to walk with Him "in the light of His Word," and the blueprint for the tabernacle was to prepare them for a life of worship.

It is therefore significant that for many in today's Judeo-Christian world, worship doesn't come to mind when they think of Sinai. For many, Sinai is simply the place of the giving of the law. But the giving of the law represents only half of what God did at Sinai. The other half is the revelation of the pattern for the building of the tabernacle—to the end that Israel would do what He had said they would do on that mountain—worship Him.

Much could be said at this juncture about the need to balance the law (Word) and the tabernacle (worship), or Word and Spirit, which is what this dual emphasis at Sinai is intended to teach us, but that is broadly treated in an earlier chapter. However, suffice to say that there are churches that have camped at the foot of Mount Sinai for much of their history through an emphasis on the importance of the law (particularly the Ten Commandments), all the while missing the other half of what God revealed there. This leads to a warped or imbalanced spirituality, for "the letter kills, but the Spirit gives life" (2 Corinthians 3:6).

Furthermore, God never wastes an illustration, and since the purpose of the tabernacle was for the worship of God, which Moses was to build exactly according to the pattern God showed him ("And let them make Me a sanctuary, that I may dwell among them. According to all that I show you, that is, the pattern of the tabernacle and the pattern of all its furnishings, just so you shall make it," Exodus 25:8, 9), it therefore follows that the blueprint for the construction of the tabernacle reveals the pattern for the worship God desires from His people. So let's watch this pattern emerge as we take a quick walk through the tabernacle.

THE TABERNACLE

Known as the tent of meeting (Exodus 39:32), it was divided into three main parts: 1) the outer area, or courtyard, surrounded by a linen curtain, 2) the first area inside the wooden structure known as the Holy Place, and 3) the area beyond the Holy Place separated by an ornate veil, known as the Holy of Holies (or Most Holy Place). Entry into the second and third areas was restricted to those carrying out the priestly service. Scripture reveals the various pieces of furnishings that adorned the tabernacle and the order in which they were to be arranged.

Altar of Burnt Offering (Exodus 27:1-8)

The altar of burnt offering, also known as the brazen altar, on which spotless lambs and goats were offered as sacrifice (or "sin offering"), was the first place or object one would encounter upon entering the tent, a reminder to New Testament Christians that entry into the Lord's presence is made possible solely through the sacrifice of the spotless Lamb, Jesus. Pure worship begins with an accurate understanding of what qualifies us to come into God's presence in the first place—faith in the grace and forgiveness of the Lamb who was slain for our sins before the very foundation of the world. **In this part of the tabernacle, the heart cry of the true worshipper should be "Behold, the Lamb!"**

Laver (Exodus 30:18-21)

The second piece of furniture was the laver, a basin used by the priests for washing. The essence of God's instructions regarding the laver in Exodus 30:18-21 is that one has to be clean to serve. This is echoed in the well-known verses from Psalm 24: "Who may ascend into the hill of the Lord? Or who may stand in His holy place? He who has clean hands and a pure heart, who has not lifted up his soul to an idol, nor sworn deceitfully" (vv. 3, 4). Our sins have been forgiven, but we still live in the flesh, we still get dirt on our hands and in our hearts. Our being justified freely by faith in Christ doesn't negate the need for ongoing sanctification. **So the laver is the place of purity, symbolic of the worshipper's heart cry: "Purify my heart."**

Table of Showbread (Exodus 25:23-30)

The table of showbread, also made of gold, stood directly opposite the golden lampstand. Each week the priests placed twelve freshly baked loaves of bread on the table of showbread, displayed there before the Lord all week, and eaten on the Sabbath. This is a beautiful picture of fellowship between God and the worshipper. The goal of the Christian life is unbroken fellowship with God, and the key to such fellowship is to feast daily on the bread of life. Not only did Jesus declare Himself the bread of life, He asserted that those who partake of Him will never hunger (John 6:35). This is why the Passover Supper was so central to the worship life of the nation of Israel, and why the Lord's Supper celebration, one of the two ordinances given to the New Testament church, holds an important place on the church's calendar. And this is why it is so sad that many remain spiritually hungry while seated at the Lord's table. The table of showbread reminds us of the importance of our fellowship and communion with Christ. **The true worshipper's heart cry should be "Bread of heaven, feed me till I want no more!"**

Lampstand *(Exodus 25:31–39)*

The next item, situated on the south side of the Holy Place, was the golden lampstand, which provided the only light in this inner section of the tent and which was to burn there perpetually. Much work went into the crafting of this very detailed lampstand, all of which has spiritual symbolism. But for our purpose, we will simply note that the Lamb, who is the object of our worship, is described in John's gospel as having light in Himself: "In Him was life, and that life is the light of men. And the light shines in the darkness, and the darkness did not comprehend it" (1:4, 5). The goal of true worship is to let the light of Jesus shine on us. We are the light of the world (Matthew 5:14), but like the moon, which has no light in itself but reflects the light of the sun, we are to be reflectors of the light that shines from the Son, Jesus. **The heart cry of the true worshipper should be "Lord, shine your light on me."**

Altar of Incense *(Exodus 30:1–10)*

In front of the veil, which separated the Holy Place from the Most Holy, was the altar of incense (made of pure gold), the third and last piece of furniture in that section of the tabernacle. Though an annual atonement was made on the horns of this altar, it was not used for the daily sacrifices. Rather, it was for the burning of special incense which created a sweet aroma to the Lord.

Describing what he saw in the apocalyptic vision, John wrote, "Now when He had taken the scroll, the four living creatures and the twenty-four elders fell down before the Lamb, each having a harp, and golden bowls full of incense, which are the prayers of the saints" (Revelation 5:8). The altar of incense is therefore symbolic of the place where prayers are made. In the worship of heaven, prayer is no small matter, and neither should it be in our worship here on earth. Prayer is worship, and worship is prayer. Worship is a lifestyle, lived daily through ongoing prayers of praise and petition. That's why in that epic encounter with the money-changers in the temple, Jesus declared, "My house shall be called a house of prayer..." (Matthew 21:13). **The heart cry of a true worshipper should therefore be, "Lord, make me an offering of worship to You, a sweet aroma that flows from unbroken fellowship and communion."**

Ark of the Covenant and the Mercy Seat *(Exodus 25:10–22)*

The ark of the covenant, also known as the ark of the testimony, and the mercy seat, are the last two pieces of furnishings in the tabernacle, situated in the Most Holy Place, God's "inner sanctum," His immediate presence. No doubt this is the reason the ark and mercy seat have come to symbolize the very presence of God. Much time could be spent on the symbolic meaning of the items which God later commanded Moses to place in the ark: the Ten Commandments, the pot of manna, and Aaron's rod which budded. But for now, the pattern for worship that emerges from the ark and mercy seat is the recognition of God's covenant (commitment) to His people, the faithfulness of His promise and provision, and the abundance of His grace and mercy. Perhaps this is what the writer to the Hebrews had in mind when he wrote, "Let us therefore come boldly to the throne of grace, that we may obtain mercy and find grace to help in time of need" (Hebrews 4:16). To truly worship God is to be lost in the wonder of His covenant love and abundant mercy. **God's amazing love, the newness and freshness of His daily mercies, symbolic of His great faithfulness, should be the heart cry of the true worshipper.**

PUTTING IT ALL TOGETHER

In summary, worship is contemplating the slain Lamb, our sufficient sacrifice. Worship is the purifying of the heart with the water of the Spirit. Worship is taking the very life of God into us by eating of the Bread of Life, which alone satisfies the soul. Worship is to walk in the light of God's presence, to be totally transparent before Him who is the light of the world and who calls us to reflect His light to the world around us. Worship is prayer, communion, and fellowship with God. And worship is being lost in the breathless wonder of God's amazing love and mercy. This pattern of worship is observed in the layout and furnishings of the Old Testament tabernacle. It paints a pattern that follows this sequence: contemplation, purification, satisfaction, reflection, communion, and wonder. The end result of worship is to be lost in the wonder of the One we worship, as the last line of the classic hymn, "Love Divine, All Loves Excelling," underscores: "Till we cast our crowns before Thee, lost in wonder, love, and praise." If you long to be lost in the breathless wonder of our Lord, linger in His presence, and order your worship after this pattern.

A LIMITED VIEW

This chapter would be incomplete without a reminder about the limitations of the tabernacle system. The author of Hebrews devotes considerable time outlining the compartments and furnishings of the tabernacle and the service of the priesthood, reminding his readers that as beautiful as these things were, they represent a system of worship that was limited because it wasn't able to affect the conscience and heart of the worshipper: "...the Holy Spirit indicating this, that the way into the Holiest of All was not yet made manifest while the first tabernacle was still standing. It was symbolic for the present time in which both gifts and sacrifices are offered which cannot make him who performed the service perfect in regard to the conscience..." (9:8, 9). That's why the veil of the temple was rent in two at the time of Jesus' crucifixion, signifying the cessation of the old system and the beginning of the new. The greatest difference between the old and the new is Jesus. In the Old Testament the tabernacle is God's dwelling place, but through Christ who tabernacles with us, God's dwelling place in the New Testament is in believers and in the church. So may the pattern of the Old Testament tabernacle always point us to Jesus. May we, through Him, be a living holy tabernacle.

REVIEW QUESTIONS

1. What is God's grand objective in redeeming the nation of Israel out of Egyptian bondage?

2. How does pure worship begin? That is, what qualifies us to come into God's presence?

3. Why is ongoing sanctification important?

4. What is the goal of the Christian life and the key to realizing this goal?

5. What is the effect of Christ's light on true worshippers?

6. How does God symbolize the fellowship of prayer?

7. What is a pattern of worship that emerges from the ark and the mercy seat?

8. What are the six components of the pattern of worship observed in the tabernacle?

APPLICATION QUESTIONS

1. What are the characteristics that accompany being in awe of something? What does being "in awe of" look and feel like?

2. The tabernacle was constructed as an "awe-inspiring" place, that awe might permeate the very atmosphere of worship. Which of the characteristics that you listed above most regularly describe your own worship?

3. It is fairly easy to imagine the visual impact of the tabernacle. How did the tabernacle engage the other senses in this pattern of worship?

    a. What were the sounds?

    b. How did it smell?

    c. How was the sense of taste engaged?

    d. What elements would be touched? What did they feel like?

4. Consider the six components in the pattern of worship observed in the tabernacle. Which of these *most* strongly characterize your worship? Which of these *least* strongly characterize your worship?

5. Note the element of the tabernacle that least strongly characterizes your worship. Set a timer for three minutes, and close your eyes while picturing yourself at this location of the tabernacle. What do you see, hear, smell, etc.? When the time is up, reflect on what you experienced and how you might incorporate this piece of the pattern into your daily worship.

Endnotes

Scripture quotations were taken from the *New King James Version.*

CHAPTER 16

DESIGNING DYNAMIC WORSHIP SERVICES

Corporate worship should be dynamic and life-changing, not mediocre and boring, and such worship doesn't just happen, but results from deliberate and purposeful planning.

After reading this chapter, you will be able to

- describe the significance of weekly worship planning and evaluation;
- list three steps for conducting evaluations of worship services;
- list the four "acts" of a worship service;
- describe the purpose and benefits of evaluating worship services;
- list eight keys to designing dynamic worship services.

Coming to Him as to a living stone, rejected indeed by men, but chosen by God and precious, you also, as living stones, are being built up a spiritual house, a holy priesthood, to offer up spiritual sacrifices acceptable to God through Jesus Christ (1 Peter 2:4, 5).

"Worship is the missing jewel in modern evangelicalism."[1]

T he importance and priority of worship demand that careful attention be given to designing the weekly worship service. Worship is more than a weekly corporate event, but what we do together corporately can enhance what we do individually and privately. Therefore, worship that is well planned and executed does more for the cause of the kingdom than many realize. *If corporate worship is truly a meeting between God and His people, how the worship service is designed is critical as to whether or not that meeting actually happens.* Worship that is poorly designed can affect people's disposition toward God, as the following quote illustrates: "When I was a boy, the thought of heaven used to frighten me more than the thought of hell. I pictured heaven as a place where time would be perpetual Sundays with perpetual services from which there would be no escape....It was a horrible nightmare...and made me an atheist for ten years."[2]

Beneficial as it is, however, deliberate weekly worship planning, let alone regular evaluation of it, does not take place in many congregations. The thought of planning and evaluation is intimidating for many. Some have never really grasped its importance and benefits. Others figure that if attendance and giving are okay, worship must be doing well. There are still others who aren't prepared to pay the price of regular planning and honest evaluation, so they settle for the status quo, whether consciously or subconsciously.

But corporate worship deserves far better. It deserves the investment of quality time and prayer that makes for a dynamic and invigorating worship experience. At its core, worship is about God, so making worship a priority is making God priority, giving our utmost for His highest. This chapter is aimed at offering small but concrete steps in that direction. Let's consider them.

KEYS TO DESIGNING DYNAMIC WORSHIP SERVICES

First, view worship planning as the most important activity of the week.

Worship isn't just another activity on the weekly church calendar; it is the church's most important activity of the week. Daily ministry and witness should anticipate the climactic celebration of the gathered community at the end of the week. This should influence the quality of time and attention devoted to worship planning and preparation. According to Eugene Peterson, this should move worship to the top of the pastor's list of weekly priorities: "The most important thing a pastor does is stand in a pulpit every Sunday and say, 'Let us worship God.' If that ceases to be the primary thing I do in terms of my energy, my imagination, and the way I structure my life, then I no longer function as a pastor."[3]

But this prioritization isn't confined to the pastor; it applies to all involved in worship. Viewing worship as the most important activity of the week will greatly increase the dedication and heart commitment of those involved, which increases the blessings that flow from such efforts.

Second, meet regularly for worship planning and prayer.

Many worship teams get together weekly to go over the music package for the upcoming service. Such gatherings typically involve reviewing the song selection, a quick prayer, and rehearsal. This may be as much as can be expected, given the busy lives team members lead. Turning every worship team gathering into an extended prayer meeting and evaluation session is unrealistic. Worship practitioners therefore recommend additional meetings such as annual retreats, quarterly and monthly meetings, and other impromptu gatherings during which attention can be given to worship matters not usually focused on during weekly rehearsals. These various meetings will involve different circles of people beyond the worship team—sound and tech crew, pastoral staff, etc. Done effectively, these meetings will yield tremendous benefits over the long term.

But the benefits that come from these special meetings throughout the year are no substitute for the benefits to be derived from time taken during the regular weekly meetings for quick evaluation. In fact, it's been suggested that worship teams meet for a few minutes immediately following each service while the experience is still fresh on everyone's mind, for so much gets lost by the time the team meets the following week. Here are three simple steps for conducting brief but regular evaluations:

1. *Review.* Before the team looks ahead to the upcoming service, it should take a few minutes to look back at the service just past. This may take the form of a brief review or critique (highs and lows, team members' observations, comments from those in the congregation, etc.) or by use of a standard set of questions that reflect the core values of the team. Here's an example, based on Bob Kauflin and C. J. Mahaney's "Ten Questions for Evaluating Worship."[4] There, the list is titled "Preparing for and Evaluating the Worship Service."

   Are the various elements of our worship anchored in Scripture?

   Does our worship reflect the gospel; does it point worshippers to Jesus?[5]

   Does our order of worship and song selection reflect a clear theme and direction?

   Has our worship become predictable?

   Do we leave room for the spontaneous redirection of the Holy Spirit?

   If done on a regular basis, asking such questions should only take a relatively short period of time. Each worship team should craft its own short and long lists for use in ongoing evaluations.

2. *Devotion and Prayer.* Having looked backward, it's time to look upward in prayer. There should be a time of prayer that goes beyond thanksgiving for safe travels to the meeting place. Time constraints prohibit making an extended prayer meeting out of the weekly gatherings, but prayer must be more than a perfunctory exercise. A time of prayer should follow a brief devotional thought provided either by the lead member of the team or by the pastor. The pastor may be present because he is part of the team or because of his pastoral care commitment to the team. If the pastor is present and is the speaker for the upcoming service, his devotional thoughts may be based on his message. This not only sets

the tone for focused prayer, it casts a vision for the coming service. In this way, bathing the service in prayer flows more naturally.

3. *Worship Planning.* The team is now ready to craft the order and content of the service. In *Worship: Old & New*, noted worship teacher, the late Robert E. Webber, suggests that the service be viewed as a play or drama with several "acts" or "movements." Essentially, the worship service should be a reenactment of the drama of redemption. So in terms of service content, Webber outlines four acts (or segments): (i) the assembly, (ii) listening and responding, (iii) remembering and giving, and (iv) going forth to love and serve.[6]

In the assembly portion of the service, worshippers are reminded that they are the people of God, that they have come to the house of God where He is present and desires to speak to them as His gathered community, and that their hearts are to be made ready to hear and respond. Specific elements which may be included are: call to worship, greeting, invocation, praise, silence and meditation, etc.

The listening and response segment centers on the proclamation of the Word. This includes the (public) reading of Scripture, worship around the Scripture reading, and the climactic point of the service during which God speaks to the people. In more formal settings, the people respond to the Word by standing and reciting a written creed or statement of the church followed by singing. In our contemporary setting, the general way of responding to the proclamation of the Word is through a time of singing (hymn, gospel song, or worship chorus).

Webber's third "act" (remembering and giving thanks) includes the celebration of the Eucharist. As a way of "remembering" and gratefully celebrating the story of redemption, churches vary in how frequently they share in communion. However, even if the Eucharist is not celebrated weekly, there are ways through which Christ's "redemptive act" may be highlighted regularly through creative Scripture reading, music, drama and storytelling. The goal of remembering is to evoke gratitude. The word Eucharist shares a common root with familiar words such as thanks, grace, and gift—words and concepts essential to dynamic worship.

The final "act" in Webber's outline is the "going forth" of the faith community. They've gathered and worshipped around the Word, and have gratefully reflected on the story of redemption. It is now time to point them outward, to prepare them to "Lift high the cross, the love of Christ proclaim, till all the world adore His sacred name" (to borrow the first stanza of a classic hymn). This is the missional purpose of the church, emphasized in this final segment of the service. We enter to worship and we depart to serve. In this sense, the "service" really begins after the benediction. Different worshippers will remember different parts of the service, but usually all remember how the service ends. The closing song, prayer, benediction (pronouncement of a blessing), and the recessional are therefore as important as the opening and call to worship.

Third, aim at offering acceptable worship.

Second to the question of how one is saved or justified before God, the most important question Christians can ask is, "How shall we worship?" Scripture provides one right answer to this question. Consider these references:

> I beseech you therefore, brethren, by the mercies of God, that you present your bodies a living sacrifice, holy, acceptable to God, which is your reasonable service (Romans 12:1).

> Therefore, since we are receiving a kingdom which cannot be shaken, let us have grace, by which we may serve God acceptably with reverence and godly fear. For our God is a consuming fire (Hebrews 12: 28, 29).

> Coming to Him as to a living stone, rejected indeed by men, but chosen by God and precious, you also, as living stones, are being built up a spiritual house, a holy priesthood, to offer up spiritual sacrifices acceptable to God through Jesus Christ (1 Peter 2:4, 5).

The common thread in these references is the word *acceptable*, underscoring God's demand that we worship Him on His terms, not ours. This demand for acceptable worship and humanity's tendency to offer what is less than acceptable goes all the way back to the beginning of the human family. This is illustrated in the tragic account in Genesis 4. The take-away from the story of Cain and Abel is that what makes worship acceptable or unacceptable is the attitude of the worshipper's heart. Worship that God accepts is that which is offered humbly in faith, proceeding from a heart and attitude rightly aligned with God.

No one argues with God's demand for acceptable worship, no one complains that such demand is unreasonable. Yet we fail to meet this standard on a regular basis. The challenge lies in the fact that we live in a culture given to self-gratification, convenience, and egalitarianism. Such mindset is driven by what works, what feels good, what's trendy; it subtly pushes God's desire for acceptable worship to the sidelines. We must therefore resolutely determine to worship God on His terms, not ours. We must offer worship from the heart, inspired by the Spirit of God, not driven by the spirit of the age.

Fourth, view all elements of the service as worship.

Worship is greatly enhanced when all elements of the service are viewed as worship. For example, the tendency to think of the offering as something to be gotten out of the way so we can get to the important elements of worship creates dichotomies in people's minds that are unnecessary and, in some instances, unbiblical. We worship through giving our tithes and offerings. The goal of giving is to inspire us to offer up our very lives. Worship should prepare the congregation for the message, but worship is more than preparation for the message. Worship is the message; the message is worship. If worship is conversation between God and His people, then Scripture reading (God's Word to us) and prayer (our communion with God) is worship. All elements of the service should be viewed as worship.

Fifth, view worship as enhancing the glory of God.

It's been said that the end goal of worship is to make God beautiful. Some would argue that we cannot make God beautiful for God's beauty is intrinsic; we cannot add to nor subtract from it. But there is universal agreement among Christians that the chief end of humanity is to glorify God. This is the focus of the very first question in the Westminster Shorter Catechism. Since our chief aim in all of life is to glorify God, and since God's divine attribute called "glory" speaks of the radiance and splendor that emanates from His very being, the frequent scriptural command to glorify God involves making God beautiful. We make God beautiful by putting His glory on display. This thought is beautifully captured in this quote by John Piper: "God created us for this: to live our lives in a way that makes Him look more like the greatness and the beauty and the infinite worth that He really is. This is what it means to be created in the image of God."[7]

As God's image-bearers, we must view worship as putting God's glory and beauty on display. We must continually raise the standard and quality of our worship to match the beauty of the worship of heaven. Let us therefore be committed to beauty and excellence in worship, to give to the Lord the glory He deserves. This is the purpose and goal of worship.

Sixth, handle music with care and wisdom.

Music ranks near the top of all elements of corporate worship. Second to the sermon, it is the worshipper's biggest take-away. So to put it succinctly, if the music isn't done right, the service flops like a cake that has no flour.

The food analogy is helpful because music is said to be "the food of life." If we treat music the way we should treat food we would pay close attention to what makes for a healthy and unhealthy music diet, understand food groups (which types of foods go together and which do not), and keep in mind what restaurant connoisseurs understand—the relationship between plate and palate. How food looks on the plate (the presentation) can affect how it appeals to the taste buds.

Therefore, avoid unhealthy choices; select healthy music. Value variety; avoid too much of the same thing. If music is the food of life, variety is its spice. So avoid inappropriate placement of songs. Some songs don't go together; some do not belong at a particular place in the service. If worship is all about ascribing worth to our sovereign God, "Shall We Gather at the River?" and "I Must Tell Jesus" do not belong at the beginning of the service or qualify for call to worship. These old gospel songs are beautiful and have their place, but we must be careful to put them in their right place. So, is your music disjointed or out of place? By all means, avoid singing that is off-pitch and distorted. Just because someone loves to sing doesn't qualify them to be a member of the worship team. It is better to not have a worship team than to have one that's painful to the ears. As Dr. Howard Hendricks once said, "A mist in the pulpit is a fog in the pews."[8] That old saying is aimed at preachers, but it's also good for worship teams. Musically, a mist in the worship team creates deep fog in the congregation. So handle music with care and wisdom.

Seventh, prepare the heart.

Now that the stage is set and all are in place, it's time to prepare the heart. This is instructional for the worship team as well as the congregation. It is possible to miss worship while attempting to lead others in it, and it is also possible for congregants to arrive at church so frazzled that they miss the "God encounter." Add to that the many distractions common to our day such as cell phones, texts, etc., and the odds are stacked against us when it comes to undistracted worship. That's why deliberate preparation is tantamount. It will not totally prevent distraction and interruption, but it can help us better handle them.

Thankfully, the principle of preparation is firmly anchored in Scripture. God's instructions to Israel regarding the observance of the Sabbath include setting aside the day prior to the Sabbath as a day of preparation ("Now when evening had come, because it was the Preparation Day, that is, the day before the Sabbath...," Mark 15:42). For Israel, it was a reminder that meeting with God was no small matter. They were about to meet with a holy God who demands to be treated as holy, so preparation is necessary. It was an opportunity to refocus, to empty the heart of life's stuff, and prepare for meeting with God.

Few of us are able to devote an entire day for preparation. But all of us can carve out time and develop a workable method for preparing the heart. Spend time consecrating your heart to the Lord in prayer, and impress upon the congregation to do the same. The question, "Who may dwell in Your holy hill?" (Psalm 15:1) is a question for those who stand between God and His people—leaders, worship teams, etc. This entire Psalm can serve as a mirror in getting ready for church. Spend time in private worship. The level of our private devotion determines the level of our public worship. Preparation makes for holy anticipation, and greatly increases the potential for dynamic worship.

Eighth, regularly evaluate your worship.

To play off of a well-known colloquialism, this final key to designing dynamic worship may be boiled down to the phrase "evaluate, evaluate, evaluate." We talked about evaluation earlier in this chapter, but an overarching vision still needs to be cast regarding its importance. One of the greatest threats to dynamic worship is the failure to make evaluation a normal part of the worship culture of the congregation. To evaluate worship is to ask honest questions such as,

How are we doing?

Why do we do what we do?

What must we change in order to remain fresh and dynamic?

To ask such questions can be awkward because it requires confronting aspects of our worship that have either become routine or untouchable, or are on their way to becoming such. However, because of the importance and priority of worship, nothing should be allowed to become untouchable. It's been noted that the first sign of institutionalism is when preserving and protecting the organization takes priority over commitment to the purpose for the organization's existence. When that happens, few, if any, dare to ask the tough questions. We must therefore guard against spiritual atrophy. We must make evaluation a core value.

Furthermore, evaluation of our worship should go beyond questions about the previous service to attitudes and relationships. Are we frustrating one another, perhaps unintentionally? In the daily grind of ministry, misunderstandings occur, expectations go unmet, and people's feelings get hurt. Making sure all is well is vital to the spiritual health and unity of the team, and can avert outright rifts in relationships as well as those quiet undercurrents that result from hurt feelings left unaddressed over long periods.

Consider also that a good bit of evaluation does take place following the weekly worship service. It happens spontaneously in the church parking lot, on the drive home, or at the dinner table. This is the only evaluation that takes place in most congregations. But that ought not to be. Let's commit to something better. Since evaluation happens anyway, let's influence how it happens. Let's make it deliberate, constructive, and done in a way that makes the greatest difference and yields the best results. To that end, the following list of benefits of worship evaluation is offered as a fitting conclusion to this chapter. This list is drawn from *Designing Worship Together*, by Norma deWaal Malefyt and Howard Vanderwell, in the chapter on "Worship Evaluation."[9]

- Those who serve well need encouragement. Most worship leaders wonder if others appreciate their efforts. How healthy, then, to have a forum where leaders can be affirmed for their good efforts.
- Evaluation will encourage the development of thoughtful and wise practices. Healthy practices must be reinforced until they are ingrained. When someone says, "Be sure to do this again," good

practices are reinforced. Many good evaluations have "for next time" written all over them.

- Evaluation will balance out the negative criticism that is easily made. Complaints come so easily. We all hear them. A thoughtful plan for evaluation will draw out the positive comments also.
- Evaluation can stir the leader's creativity and motivation. People who speak from their heart will enable leaders to view worship through the eyes of the broader congregation.
- Evaluation will enhance seasonal worship planning. When planning for one season, it's helpful to review the notes taken on worship during that season last year. Learning from the previous years prompts an annual growth process.
- Evaluation provides a healthy corrective in planning. It's easy for slight shifts over a period of time to get us off track unintentionally or to get stuck in a rut. A healthy evaluation process catches such shifts and enables us to make the necessary correctives.
- Evaluations remind us that our work is not about us. True, egos can get humbled in the evaluation process. Though quite painful at times, this can be good. Our efforts are not for ourselves but for the larger cause of giving glory to God and edifying the congregation.
- Intentional evaluation can be a safeguard against hyper-evaluation. Some evaluations are too soon and too harsh. A thoughtful and intentional process will promote growth, not pain.

AN IMPORTANT REMINDER

Prescribing a specific order of service is not the goal of this chapter. The specifics of the service will depend on particular styles and customs unique to each local setting. Rather, the goal is to offer a general framework on which a dynamic worship experience can be built. Like the frame of a house, it needs walls, windows, doors, and those things that make it livable. You've been given a frame on which to build a house of praise and worship. It is now the task of each worship team to complete it, to fill in the details, to plan dynamic worship.

REVIEW QUESTIONS

1. What is the significance of weekly worship planning and evaluation? Why is it important?

2. List three steps for conducting evaluations of worship services.

3. According to Webber, what are the four "acts" of a service?

4. What are the purposes and benefits of evaluating worship services?

5. List eight keys to designing dynamic worship services.

APPLICATION QUESTIONS

1. Does worship planning currently have the highest priority of anything on the church calendar? What activities are given higher precedence? How can your church calendar be adjusted to prioritize worship planning? Consider the schedules of the members of the worship team and other church activities in which they are involved.

2. Each worship team should craft its own short and long lists for use in ongoing evaluations. Identify five questions that would be meaningful evaluation tools for your worship team.

3. Consider the four "acts" of a worship service. Give examples of how your service currently covers each of these acts. Are any "acts" missing or out of balance?

4. List every element of your current worship service (songs, announcements, prayer requests, offerings, etc.) How are you currently framing

each of these elements as an act of worship? How can these acts of worship be made more intentional?

5.   Gather your song sets from the past four weeks of worship services.

6.   Are the opening songs focused on ascribing worth to God?

7.   How well are the themes of each song connected to one another?

8.   Repetition is key to familiarity and participation, but variety plays an important role in connecting with more members of the congregation. How many genres of music are represented in your song sets?

9.   Look at each of the eight keys of designing dynamic worship services. List five action points to discuss with your worship team.

Endnotes

Scripture quotations are from the *New King James Version*.

1.   A. W. Tozer, *The Best of A. W. Tozer* (Grand Rapids: Baker Book House, 1978), 217, as quoted in the Rosses Ministry Bible Studies (http://rosses.servingwithjoy.com/biblestudies/missingjewel2.html). Web accessed 9-10-15.
2.   Lloyd George, quoted in *One Man"s Odyssey*, by Ian Pearce, MD (Random House UK, 1986), 273.
3.   Eugene Peterson, quoted in *Leadership Journal* (Spring 1997), www.christianitytoday.com/le/1997/spring/71220a.html. Web accessed 6-23-15.
4.   Worship Matters (http://www.worshipmatters.com/2006/12/15/worship-leaders-pastors-preparing-for-and-evaluating-the-worship-service/. Web accessed 6-23-15.
5.   Question added by Whaid Rose.
6.   Robert E. Webber, *Worship: Old & New Revised Edition* (Grand Rapids: Zondervan, 1994), 153–189.
7.   John Piper, quoted in http://www.goodreads.com/quotes/242097-god-created-us-for-this-to-live-our-lives-in. Web accessed 6-23-15.
8.   Howard Hendricks, quoted in www.missionfrontiers.org/issue/article/the-measure-of-a-ministry. Web accessed 6-23-15.
9.   Norma deWaal Malefyt and Howard Vanderwell, *Designing Worship Together* (Herndon: Alban Institute, 2005) 153–176.

CHAPTER 17

LONGING FOR THE PRESENCE OF THE LORD

The Lord's presence isn't a good luck charm to be manipulated for personal benefit. Rather, it is to be experienced as a matter of the heart, informed by timeless biblical principles about the Lord's presence.

After reading this chapter, you will be able to

- identify three reasons for longing for the Lord's presence;
- identify what the ark of the covenant symbolized;
- list four principles in rightly relating to God's presence;
- describe two symbolic actions to take in rightly relating to God's presence.

In Your presence is fullness of joy;
At Your right hand are pleasures forevermore (Psalm 16:11).

"Current evangelicalism has...laid the altar and divided the sacrifice into parts, but now seems satisfied to count the stones and rearrange the pieces with never a care that there is not a sign of fire upon [the] top of lofty Carmel."[1]

T he book *The Pursuit of God* is described as one of the finest works to come from the pen of A. W. Tozer—late pastor, scholar, Christian statesman, and one of the most prolific writers of the previous century. In the Introduction, Dr. Samuel Zwemer describes it as "a masterly study of the inner life."[2] I concur. It is one of the most impacting books I've ever read.

In the preface to this volume, Tozer reflects on what he calls "the only real harbinger of revival"[3] visible anywhere on the religious horizon:

> In this hour of all-but-universal darkness, one cheering gleam appears:
> within the fold of conservative Christianity there are to be found
> increasing numbers of persons whose religious lives are marked by a
> growing hunger after God Himself. They are eager for spiritual realities
> and will not be put off with words, nor will they be content with correct
> "interpretations" of truth. They are athirst for God, and they will not be
> satisfied till they have drunk deep at the Fountain of Living Water.[4]

Though written more than a half century ago, these words speak directly to our twenty-first century context. And nowhere in the life and ministry of the church is this hunger and thirst for God more distinctly manifested than in the area of worship. We long for the Lord's presence for three reasons. First, because we can't help ourselves—because of the way we were created. According to Solomon, in Ecclesiastes 3:11, God has put eternity in our hearts. Theologians call this the "imago dei," Latin for "the image of God." Created in God's image, humans have an innate sense of a divine or supernatural being. This explains why worship is said to be "universal in its appeal and practice," meaning that all peoples and cultures worship. They may worship gods of wood and stone, but they worship nonetheless. Second, we long for God's presence because of what it affords us: "In your presence is fullness of joy; at your right hand are pleasures forevermore" (Psalm 16:11). David elaborates further on the benefits of God's presence in the familiar 23rd Psalm by use of words such as *comfort*, *protection*, and *guidance*. And third, we long for the Lord's presence because it confirms our walk with Him and validates ministry. Smoke on the mountain, the pillar of cloud by day and pillar of fire by night, the *shekinah* glory of the Lord that frequently filled the tabernacle (so much so that no one could enter it), confirmed the presence of the Lord among His people as they journeyed through the wilderness. And such confirmation is sought even in our journey as New Testament pilgrims.

Such confirmation is what God's people were missing when the story opens in 1 Samuel 4. For context, this is the period of transition from the era of the judges to the era of the kings. The familiar verse "In those days there was no king in Israel; everyone did what was right in his own eyes" (Judges 21:25) describes this time period. We also read in 1 Samuel 3:1 that "the word of the Lord was rare in those days; there was no widespread revelation." That a serious spiritual breach existed within the leadership of Israel is therefore no surprise. Eli's sons, Hophni and Phinehas, committed open acts of fornication and corruption (1 Samuel 2:22). As a result, the Israelites lived under the constant attack of their arch enemy, the Philistines.

We come now to Chapter 4 which records two battles between Israel and the Philistines. At the end of the first battle, 4,000 Israeli fighters lay dead on the battlefield (see v. 2). In verse 3 the elders of Israel speculated as to the reason they lost the battle. Concluding that it's because the ark of the covenant was not in their midst when they went into battle, they set out to retrieve the ark which, at that time, was in Shiloh.

This raises an important question: What's the big deal about the ark? Essentially, the ark had come to symbolize God's very presence. God's instructions for the furnishing of the tabernacle include the construction of a chest (or box) that would contain items that represent God's covenant dealings with Israel, to be placed in the Holy of Holies. It was covered with gold and had a lid, or "mercy seat," on top surrounded by two cherubs with outstretched wings. The cherubs on top of the ark were artificial, but they symbolized angelic creatures whose sole purpose is the unceasing praise and worship of God. Israel had come to believe that God lives between these two cherubs (or *cherubim*): "So the people sent to Shiloh, that they might bring from there the ark of the covenant of the Lord of hosts, who dwells between the cherubim" (1 Samuel 4:4). You may read additional details concerning the ark in Exodus 25:10–21.

But a curious thing happens in the verses that follow. Israel is attacked by the Philistines a second time, and though the ark is in their midst, they are sorely defeated once again, suffering 30,000 casualties, the capture of the ark by the Philistines, and the death of Eli's two sons. News of the defeat and devastation was too much for Eli; he died of a heart attack. And it caused Phinehas's wife, who was pregnant, to go into labor. She died during child-birth, but not before naming her son: "Then she named the child Ichabod, saying, "The glory has departed from Israel!" (v. 21).

This brings us to the end of Chapter 4 where things aren't going well for the Israelites. That which had come to symbolize God's very presence, that on which they had come to depend for victory over their enemy, was now in the hands of their enemy. And because the Philistines were well aware of what the ark meant to the Israelites, they placed it in the temple of Dagon, chief among their gods, to gain whatever favor may result. But the following morning Dagon was found face down on the ground. Wanting to prove to themselves that there was nothing to it, they returned Dagon to its upright position. But the next day Dagon was not only fallen down again, his head and arms were broken off. This made them suspicious that having possession of the ark was rather to their disadvantage, so they began to devise a plan by which to rid themselves of it. The ark was taken to various Philistines cities, but it brought destruction wherever it was taken—the people were struck with boils and tumors. The devastation at Ekron is described in the following way at the end of chapter 5: "Therefore they sent the ark of God to Ekron. So it was, as the ark of God came to Ekron, that the Ekronites cried out, saying, 'They have brought the ark of the God of Israel to us, to kill us and our people!'" (v. 10).

So they sent and gathered together all the lords of the Philistines, and said, "Send away the ark of the God of Israel, and let it go back to its own place, so that it does not kill us and our people." For there was a deadly destruction throughout all the city; the hand of God was very heavy there. And the men who did not die were stricken with the tumors, and the cry of the city went up to heaven" (vv. 11, 12).

SPIRITUAL LESSONS

Several spiritual lessons begin to emerge at this point in the story as we explore how to rightly relate to the Lord's presence. The ark had come to symbolize God's presence, but it didn't do for Israel what they thought it would, and neither did it do any good for the Philistines. Here, then, are some of the lessons we glean from this account:

- God's presence is not a good luck charm or "Genie in a bottle."
- God's presence cannot be manufactured or manipulated.
- None of us has a monopoly on God's presence.
- There's a difference between symbol and reality.

Israel's defeat on the battlefield with the ark in their midst was to teach them that the presence of the Lord wasn't a magical power to be used at will for their protection or benefit. The ark was a *symbol* of God's presence, not the *reality* of it. In and of themselves, symbols aren't bad or evil. It's what we make of them that can be sinful. Israel had turned this symbol, the box which God told Moses to make, into an idol. They substituted the symbol for the reality, and some believers make the same mistake still today.

RIGHTLY APPROPRIATING THE LORD'S PRESENCE

So the question before us now is this: *How should Christians rightly relate to the Lord's presence?*

The following answers to this question are informed by a message by Pastor Jack Hayford heard years ago, in which he connects Israel's experience in 2 Samuel 4–6 to worship, captured in these two simple statements: 1) take it out of the box, and 2) take it off of the cart. Let's consider them.

First, take it out of the box.

This first lesson draws upon the fact that the ark was made in the shape of a box, which speaks to the tendency of Christians to make proverbial boxes in which they put spiritual things. We love boxes; what would we do without them? As one writer observes, we love boxes because they make life more manageable—keep our cereal from spilling and help us find things when we need them. If we love something and want to preserve it over time, we make a box for it and perhaps put a label on it. This is innocent until we transfer this mentality into our approach to God's presence. The God we worship is infinitely bigger than the boxes we create. The problem with boxes is that they lead to an exclusivist mentality that only tolerates those things we like and are comfortable with, and eventually to the creation of what has been called "a box-shaped deity," a god of our liking. In his poem "$3 Worth of God," Wilbur Rees captures this thought, writing that he wants just enough of God to make him comfortable—not to disturb his sleep or transform his heart toward others.

If the presence of the Lord seems elusive, it's very likely that it's been put into a box. But there's hope for those who would dare remove it. The call of the Spirit through this first point of application is therefore to take the Lord's presence out of whatever box we've put it in.

Second, take it off of the cart.

Fast forward to 2 Samuel 6 (the next book over) for the story upon which this second point of application draws. It had been twenty years since the Philistines had rid themselves of the ark. David had now ascended to the throne, and being the consummate worshipper he was, the passion of his heart was to return the ark to its rightful place. But a curious thing happened as the ark was being transported back to Jerusalem. The oxen which pulled the cart (on which the ark was being carried) stumbled, prompting Uzzah, the Levite attending the ark, to instinctively grab hold of it to stop it from falling to the ground. No doubt you know the story—he was struck dead as a result. This made David angry with the Lord, a reaction that's very much out of character for him: "And David became angry because of the Lord's outbreak against Uzzah; and he called the name of the place Perez Uzzah to this day" (2 Samuel 6:8).

David's struggle with God's action in the case of Uzzah's demise was understandable. What was God's justification for this innocent man's death? To avoid misguided speculation, consider these facts from Scripture. God had given specific instructions on how the ark was to be transported. God commanded in Exodus 25:14-15 that the ark was to be carried by the Levites on poles on their shoulders. This then raises new questions: From where did David and his men get the idea to make a cart on which to carry the ark? Were they unaware of God's instruction? Is it possible that the Levites, ardent students of the laws regarding the tabernacle, were unfamiliar with these important instructions?

Well, not likely. Instead, there's reason to believe that the idea of the cart was actually borrowed from the Philistines. The idea of transporting the ark on a cart emerged in the early verses of 1 Samuel 6 as the Philistine elders looked for a safe strategy for ridding themselves of the ark to avoid further devastation, and therein lies the basic problem with the cart. If the box represents the danger of substituting symbol for reality, the cart represents the danger of taking our spiritual cues from the enemy.

We do so by looking to the culture, rather than God's Word, for ministry strategy. To avoid misunderstanding, it should be noted that the Bible isn't anti-culture, and neither should Christians be. The gospel isn't against culture; it transcends and transforms it. We cannot impact that against which we have a reproach. The church is called to be salt and light in the world, and to do so requires getting out of the salt shaker and out from under the lampstand and into the world. But on the other hand, we must remember that the world is broken and has lost its way, making it ill-equipped to provide God's people anything of substance when it comes to spiritual instruction. So we don't look to Hollywood or Madison Avenue to determine the latest worship strategies. Jesus is building His church; He is the architect; consult Him. Take worship off of the cart.

It wasn't that David didn't know better, it was that he had come to rely on the strategy of the enemy. We can walk so closely with the world that over time we forget the obvious. Uzzah may have been sincere in his actions, but sincerity is never an acceptable substitute for obedience. God doesn't need our help; He desires our obedience. The Uzzahs of the church—sincere Christians wanting to help God out (to make things happen)—should take heed. In summary, to experience the presence of the Lord, we must 1) take it out of the box, and 2) take it off of the cart.

But as Pastor Hayford humorously underscored in his message, in the final analysis, the problem with the cart had to do with what carts are made of: "boards and big wheels." I'm sure that Dr. Hayford appreciates the role of church boards and high-ranking members of local congregations. Thank God for those who serve in such capacities with integrity and faithfulness. But most of us are familiar with the problem of boards and big wheels—

well-intended leaders whose influence is less than positive and, in some cases, destructive. That, too, can become a serious obstacle to progress in experiencing the Lord's presence.

Finally, make it a matter of the heart.

There's a third piece of instruction that must be added: Make it a matter of the heart. For the story doesn't end in 1 Samuel 6 after the ark is sent away on the cart. It continues into the next chapter which begins with these poignant words:

Then the men of Kirjath Jearim came and took the ark of the Lord, and brought it into the house of Abinadab on the hill, and consecrated Eleazar his son to keep the ark of the Lord. So it was that the ark remained in Kirjath Jearim a long time; it was there twenty years. And all the house of Israel lamented after the Lord. Then Samuel spoke to all the house of Israel, saying, "If you return to the Lord with all your hearts, then put away the foreign gods and the Ashtoreths from among you, and prepare your hearts for the Lord, and serve Him only; and He will deliver you from the hand of the Philistines (1 Samuel 7:1–3).

The ultimate solution to Israel's problem, the secret to their victory over the Philistines, was a matter of the heart—"prepare your hearts for the Lord." What does it mean to prepare one's heart for the Lord? That will be explored in the chapter that follows. Meanwhile, it serves as a present reminder that worship is a matter of the heart, that the Lord's presence cannot be manipulated or manufactured, that none of us has a monopoly on God's presence. If Tozer is right in his observation that the only real hope for spiritual revival is Christians who hunger and thirst after God, and he is, then let's take the Lord's presence out of the box and off of the cart, and make it truly a matter of the heart.

REVIEW QUESTIONS

1. What are three reasons we should long for the Lord's presence?

2. What did the ark of the covenant symbolize?

3. What are four principles for rightly relating to God's presence?

4. Describe two symbolic actions to take in rightly relating to God's presence.

APPLICATION QUESTIONS

1. What evidence in your life reflects a longing for the Lord's presence? How desperate are you to drink deeply from the fountain of Living Waters?

2. In what ways are you guilty of seeking the gifts that God gives instead of seeking God himself?

3. What is an example of a situation in which you have used prayer and worship as a "good luck charm" or to convince (manipulate) God into doing what you want Him to do?

4. What is one thing you will repent of—that is, change your mind and actions regarding—to better prepare your heart for the Lord's presence?

Endnotes

Scripture quotations are from the *New King James Version*.

1. A. W. Tozer, *The Pursuit of God* (Martino Fine Books, 2009). 7.
2. Ibid., 5.
3. Ibid., 7.
4. Ibid.

CHAPTER 18

WORSHIP: A MATTER OF THE HEART

Worship is all about Jesus Christ. Coming back to the heart of worship requires humility, emptying ourselves, aligning our hearts with God, and repenting from anything that divides us from Christ. In this place of sincere worship, we experience transformation into the image of Christ.

After reading this chapter, you will be able to

- describe the condition of the unregenerate heart;
- compare and contrast the regenerate heart with the unregenerate heart;
- explain what Samuel meant when he instructed the children of Israel to return to the Lord;
- compare and contrast pagan worship and worship of Yahweh;
- list the five words that make up the acronym HEART;

- discuss how the story of the song "Heart of Worship" assists us in focusing on Jesus in worship.

"...return to the Lord with all your heart, remove the foreign gods and the Ashtaroth from among you and direct your hearts to the Lord and serve Him alone" (1 Samuel 7:3).

"When we worship, God is looking beyond the words to our very hearts. Worship is fundamentally a matter of the heart. And worship is ultimately all about Jesus."

I n the previous chapter we reflected on what it means to long for the presence of the Lord. We looked at the beginning of 1 Samuel and drew out three main points regarding worship:

1. *Take it out of the box.* We were challenged by the question, "Do you serve a box-sized God?" We were reminded that no box can contain God. The box is a symbol of God's presence, but does not contain or limit God. We must not confuse the symbol with the reality or impose our limitations on God.
2. *Take it off of the cart.* We were challenged to stop treating God's presence the way that pagans do and start treating it as God instructed. Placing the ark on a cart represents the danger of taking our spiritual cues from the Philistines. The ark on the cart represents worship that is informed, not by the truth of God's word, but by what is trendy and popular in the culture. This is not a matter of style, but of substance.
3. *Make it a matter of the heart.* Here we left off and here we return to look at the remainder of the story in 1 Samuel. We want to ask, "What's the big deal about the heart?" and "How do we make worship a matter of the heart?" Ultimately, "How do we come back to the heart of worship?"

Scripture speaks a lot about the heart. Two passages come to mind immediately:

Watch over your heart with all diligence, for from it flow the springs of life (Proverbs 4:23).

The heart is more deceitful than all else, and is desperately sick; who can understand it? (Jeremiah 17:9).

Consider these poignant quotes from beyond the pages of Scripture:

When God measures a man, he doesn't put the tape around his head; he puts it around his heart.[1]

The heart is a perpetual factory of idols.[2]

At the heart of the human problem is the problem of the human heart.[3]

CREATE IN ME A CLEAN HEART

If all this is true of our hearts, how can we turn our hearts to worship God? The reality is that without Christ our hearts cannot be turned to God. However, when we come to new life in Christ, we are given a new heart. Of course, by "heart" we do not mean the organ beating in our chest. Rather, we're talking about our allegiances, affections, loyalties, and values. Left to ourselves these are desperately wicked, but renewed in Christ they become spiritual and good.

The battle between our heart of flesh and our spiritual heart is one that Paul speaks of in Romans 7 and Galatians 5. There is a war raging between the spirit and the flesh and the battle is being waged in our hearts. In Christ, we are able to walk according to the new, clean, regenerate heart. We can put to death the heart of flesh that would lead us down paths of destruction and death.

The condition of our heart—whether our heart is following the spirit or the flesh—is evident in our daily thoughts, words and actions. And it is evident most of all in what we offer ourselves to in worship. Worship must be understood broadly as the offering of our entire life, not just our songs. So it is that God desires every part of life to be offered to Him in worship as this reflects a heart that is turned fully toward Him.

TURN YOUR HEARTS TO THE LORD

So, let us return to 1 Samuel and explore what it means to turn our hearts to the LORD. 1 Samuel begins with the story of Samuel's ascension to the status of prophet, alongside the demise of Eli. By the end of Chapter 3, Eli has resigned himself to God's impending judgment on his family for the ways in which his sons have corrupted the worship of God.

In Chapter 4, following a defeat at the hands of the Philistines, the elders of Israel decided to take the ark of the covenant into the next battle as a good luck charm. Eli's sons are complicit in the misguided act that backfires badly on the Israelites. Despite the roar of approval in the Israelite camp upon the introduction of the ark, the Philistines carry out a great slaughter against the Israelites. Eli's sons are killed and the ark is captured.

When Eli receives the news he falls over in shock and breaks his neck, resulting in his death. His daughter-in-law responds to the news by going into premature labor and dying in the delivery of Eli's grandson, but not before naming the child Ichabod (literally "no glory") to indicate that the glory of God had departed from Israel.

But if the departure of the ark from Shiloh is bad news for the Israelites, its arrival in Ashdod is worse news for the Philistines. They bring the ark to their temple and place it before Dagon, the head of the Canaanite pantheon. Dagon falls face down before the ark on the first day, and the next day he is dismembered and lying before the ark. If the desecration of their god is not enough, the Philistines suffer from a plague. Spread by rats and fleas, the plague results in painful tumors, and a huge death count. The ark is sent from city to city, but to no avail, the plague traveled with it. Finally, the Philistines decide to return the ark to its rightful owners.

The ark eventually ends up in Kiriath-jearim after an ill-fated stop in Beth-shemesh where some Israelites had the audacity to open the ark to gaze at its sacred contents. In Kiriath-jearim the ark is supervised by a man consecrated for the purpose. This brings us to the beginning of our passage, in which the children of Israel begin to long for God and His absent presence. This longing goes on for twenty years, but to no avail. Their hearts were not yet turned to God.

And here, Samuel calls on the Israelites,

> "...return to the Lord with all your heart, remove the foreign gods and the Ashtaroth from among you and direct your hearts to the Lord and serve Him alone" (1 Samuel 7:3).

What does the prophet Samuel mean by this? Is it simply a call to serve only one God, or did it have something to do with the entire manner of worship? To answer this, we need to look below the surface of the story.

The Canaanite pantheon of gods included a deity named "Baal" who was worshiped as the storm god. As the god of rain and thunder in a primitive, agrarian society, Baal was a fertility god. The success of vegetation depended upon his approval and blessing. If he is happy, Baal gives rain and subsequently, good crops. If he is angry, he gives thunder and lightning, resulting in famine.

The fertility cult of Baal and his consort, Asherah, called upon the Philistines to engage in cultic practices—often sexual in nature—that would endear the gods to them and arouse them to engage in intercourse, bringing about the needed rain. Devotion to Baal and his consort, in the form of worship and various cult practices, as well as the erection of wooden "Asherah" poles, was therefore commonplace.

THE THEOLOGY OF MAGIC

The underlying theology of the fertility cult is a common feature of magic, both primitive and modern. In magic, the gods are understood as personal beings of great power that can be manipulated to act on behalf of humans. Indeed, if humans carry out the proper rituals, the gods are *obligated* to act in given ways.

According to the theology of magic, if people worship and serve the fertility gods faithfully then they can expect the blessing of rain. If they fail to do so, they can expect the dominance of the gods of death in the form of drought and subsequent famine. Or they can expect the displeasure of the fertility god in which he strikes them with thunder and lightning that destroy their crops.

Thus magic, in the form of the Canaanite fertility cult, is a form of worship in which the goal is for the worshipper to receive provision, protection, and pleasure. The one being worshipped is approached for what they will give in return for what is offered to them. The gods are predictable and can be manipulated by human acts.

Good fortune in life indicates the pleasure of the gods, while misfortune indicates their displeasure. The human relationship with the divine is finite and predictable, part of a closed system in which humans approach the gods in order to manipulate them for their own benefit. In the fertility cult, the ultimate goal of worship is personal/tribal wealth, health and prosperity. Thus, the center of worship is the worshipper.

THE THEOLOGY OF YAHWEH WORSHIP

This view of worship is starkly contrasted in Scripture with the worship of Yahweh. The theology of Yahweh worship rests on the knowledge that Yahweh doesn't change and cannot be manipulated by humans. In fact, the opposite is true. As is made particularly clear in the New Testament, the worship of God results in the transformation of the worshipper as the Father shapes them into the image of His Son. God is not obligated to act in response to any human act. Rather, He mercifully initiates a relationship with humanity and graciously responds when they acknowledge Him. God is infinite and unpredictable. He operates freely, unconstrained by external pressures, human or otherwise.

Thus the worship of God is fundamentally based on His incredible worth and glory. God's worshippers do not worship Him in order to receive or manipulate. Rather, they worship in order to give and be changed. Thus, one's success in this life may or may not indicate God's pleasure or displeasure. God's glory and purposes are greater than the material comfort of His creatures. And yet, God graciously blesses those who worship Him, not because they manipulate Him to do so, but because He is kind and loving.

Thus, for the covenant people of God, the ultimate goal of worshipping Him is to recognize and proclaim His great worth in recognition of His imitable attributes. And therefore, the center of worship is the one being worshipped.

WORSHIPPING WITH "ALL YOUR HEART"

With this background in mind we can now return to 1 Samuel 7 and the call of Samuel for the children of Israel to turn to Yahweh with "all your heart." The children of Israel were already lamenting, grieving terribly for the glory of the Lord to truly return to His people. This lamentation went on for twenty years! And yet, they continued to worship Baal and Asherah throughout their cities. The problem here was not as simple as idolatry or polytheism. The deeper problem was that in continuing to worship the fertility gods, the Israelites demonstrated that they did not truly understand what it meant to worship Yahweh.

The reason the elders of Israel had taken the ark into battle in Chapter 4 is because they thought of Yahweh as they thought of Baal. He was considered a good luck charm, a magic spell that could be manipulated in order to bring about a desired result. Had God allowed them to defeat the Philistines in that battle, He would have confirmed their misunderstanding. By allowing them to be defeated, He demonstrated that He was unpredictable and outside of their control. By toppling the idol of Dagon and releasing a plague, God demonstrated the same thing to the Philistines.

For the Israelites to turn to God with "all their heart" would mean embracing a new understanding of worship. They would affirm that Yahweh was not like the Canaanite deities. He was not finite and predictable, able to be manipulated. Rather, He was eternal, infinite, and all-powerful. He was deserving of worship simply because of who He was. His willingness to be gracious and merciful to those who worshipped Him was not something He was obligated to do in response to their rituals.

Thus, Samuel's call for wholehearted worship was not simply a call away from idolatry or polytheism. Rather, it was a call for the Israelites to truly worship Yahweh. In recognizing and honoring God for who He is, they would be compelled to part ways with all other "gods." They would look to God exclusively for provision, protection and peace, not because they had obligated Him through ritual, but because they trusted His promise. In short, they would stop using worship of Yahweh as a magic ritual to manipulate and receive, and would instead use it as a means to be changed and to offer themselves.

As the Israelites gathered together at Mizpah, they drew water and poured it out on the ground, a symbol of their repentance. They fasted and made the simple confession, "We have sinned against the LORD." Their sin was not primarily in worshipping other gods, but in thinking of worship in such a way that opened them to the possibility. They were now worshipping Yahweh with all their hearts, because they were worshipping Him for who He truly was.

When the Philistines heard about this gathering, they came to make war with the Israelites. Their theology of worship had not changed and they no doubt had entrusted themselves to the protection of Baal, god of thunder, and Asherah, goddess of war. It is fitting then that Yahweh rendered the

Philistines helpless that day with a powerful thunderstorm, after which the Israelites destroyed them in battle!

THE HEART OF WORSHIP

An acronym comes to mind that captures the highlights of this story from 1 Samuel 7 and what it means to worship from the heart. Let us consider this acronym:

- *Humility:* Worship begins with the humble recognition that God is God and we are not. It begins with acknowledging the greatness of God and our absolute dependence upon Him. We worship because He is worthy of all that we have and all that we are. The longing of the people after the presence of the Lord demonstrates their recognition that they are inadequate and in need of God.
- *Emptying:* Having humbled themselves, the children of Israel took water and poured it on the ground and fasted. Both the pouring of the water and the fasting symbolize a process of emptying themselves. For us to worship God with full hearts we must first be emptied of those things that distract and destruct. We must release the baggage and clutter that steals our focus and allegiance.
- *Alignment:* When we think of aligning our hearts with God, we might think of the alignment of a car. Have you ever been driving on a straight road, let go of the wheel, and noticed that the car tended to drift off the road and toward the shoulder? This phenomenon suggests that the vehicle is out of alignment. Left to itself, it will leave the straight path and end up in the ditch. So it is with our hearts, which are, as the hymn writer said, "prone to wander." We are in constant need of aligning our hearts with God's heart to keep us following hard after Him.
- *Repentance:* The word *repentance* literally means "re-thinking." It speaks to the transformation of the mind that begins with thinking new thoughts about sin and salvation and continues as our minds are trained to think the thoughts of God, rather than the thoughts of the world. We see this re-thinking taking place when the children of Israel confess their sins to God and ask Samuel to intercede on their behalf. At the heart of worship is a willingness to set our minds on the things of God, rather than on the things of this world.

- *Transformation:* The end result of worship is transformation. When Paul speaks of transformation in Romans 12:2 and 2 Corinthians 3:18, he uses the Greek word from which we derive the word *metamorphosis*. As we gaze on the face of Christ in worship, we are transformed, changed as drastically as the metamorphosis of a caterpillar to a butterfly. Worship doesn't change God; it changes us. And the change we experience is that we become more like Christ. We are transformed into His image. We see this transformation taking place in the children of Israel as they cry out to God for deliverance, rather than depending upon their own devices.

Thus we see a five-step pattern that characterizes genuine worship: Humility, Emptying, Alignment, Repentance and Transformation.

COMING BACK TO THE HEART OF WORSHIP

So, what can we say to conclude this chapter on making worship a matter of the heart? Perhaps the most fitting way in which to do so is to tell the story of one of today's most famous songs. It's a familiar story, but one worth retelling. It is the story of a church called Soul Survivor, a pastor named Mike Pilavachi, and a worship leader named Matt Redman. By the late 1990s Soul Survivor's worship ministry was receiving international acclaim for the cutting edge sound and inspiring lyrics coming out of this congregation in Watford, England. Matt Redman was becoming a household name, and the band he led was the envy of many a worship team around the world. Yet at home, there was a growing dissatisfaction among the leadership at Soul Survivor. There was a sense in which they felt that performance had replaced worship and the audience had replaced God as its focus. And so, Pastor Mike took a drastic step. He turned off the state-of-the-art PA system, fired the professional musicians, shut down the lights, and cleared the instruments off the stage.

Sometime later, Matt Redman would release a simple song about worship that he wrote in the quiet seclusion of his bedroom. This song would go on to become his most recognizable contribution to the international Christian music scene and the title track of one of his best-known albums. Over a decade later, every weekend across the world Christians gather to sing this simple song as a confession and a commitment to true worship.

The song "Heart of Worship" reminds us that worship is about far more than music. It reminds us that when we worship, God is looking beyond the words to our very hearts. Worship is fundamentally a matter of the heart. And worship is ultimately all about Jesus.

What happened to Matt Redman and the folks at Soul Survivor during that time without the elaborate production that had become such a focus of their weekly gathering? They met and offered their simple praise with sincerity of heart. Their one focus was God and His glory. With everything else stripped away, they found a place where they knew they were offering worship that was all about Jesus.

Having found that place, Soul Survivor gradually brought back the sound system and the instruments, the lights and the stage. These things were not bad in and of themselves, and with hearts in the right place they could be used to the glory of God. The folks at Soul Survivor had come back to the heart of worship. May we return to the heart of worship as well.

REVIEW QUESTIONS

1. What is the condition of the unregenerate heart?

2. How are the regenerate heart and the unregenerate heart alike? How are they different?

3. What did Samuel mean when he instructed the children of Israel to return to the LORD?

4. How are pagan worship and worship of Yahweh similar? How are they different?

5. What are the five words that make up the acronym HEART to assist us in genuine worship?

6. How does the story of the song "Heart of Worship" assist us in focusing on Jesus in worship?

APPLICATION QUESTIONS

1. In what ways does your worship of Yahweh resemble "magical"/pagan worship? Why is "magical" worship tempting to you?

2. How has God revealed Himself to you as you have read this book? Who has He revealed Himself to be?

3. How have you responded to these revelations? Compare and contrast your response to how worshippers responded throughout Scripture.

4. What baggage and clutter have distracted your heart from focusing on who God has revealed Himself to be?

5. What changes have you observed in your heart as a result of recognizing and responding to God's revelation of Himself?

6. How are you being compelled to respond right now?

Endnotes

Scripture quotations are from the *New American Standard Bible*.

1. Howard Hendricks at http://blog.godreports.com/2013/04/the-notable-and-quotable-howard-hendricks/. Web accessed 12-10-15.
2. Paraphrase of Calvin's *Institutes* (1.11.8) in John Calvin, *Institutes of the Christian Religion*, trans. Henry Beveridge (Peabody, MS: Hendrickson Publishers, 2008), 55.
3. Adrian Rogers at http://www.oneplace.com/ministries/love-worth-finding/read/articles/guard-your-heart-15291.html. Web accessed 12-10-15.

CHAPTER 19

THE GOD WE WORSHIP

God cares not only that we worship Him, but how we worship Him, and fundamental to how we worship God is our understanding of who He is.

After reading this chapter, you will be able to

- describe the relationship between true worship and an accurate understanding of God's nature and attributes;
- describe the relationship between God's imperatives and His indicatives;
- describe the role that understanding God's relationship with His Son, Jesus, plays in our understanding of God.

For it is the God who commanded light to shine out of darkness, who has shone in our hearts to give the light of the knowledge of the glory of God in the face of Jesus Christ (2 Corinthians 4:6).

"What comes into our minds when we think about God is the most important thing about us....Worship is pure or base as the worshiper entertains high or low thoughts of God. For this reason the gravest question before the Church is always God Himself, and the most portentous fact about any man is not what he at a given time may say or do, but what he in his deep heart conceives God to be like. We tend by a secret law of the soul to move toward our mental image of God."[1]

———————————

G od not only cares that we worship Him; God is very concerned about *how* we worship Him. Fundamental to how we worship God is our understanding of who God is. Part of what makes true worship true is that it is directed to the true God, and is informed by an accurate under-standing of His nature and attributes.

This is the burden of the Shema in Deuteronomy 6. Having lived in Egypt for more than four centuries, the Israelites had become quite familiar with Egypt's system of gods. It's been suggested that each of the ten plagues by which God delivered Israel out of Egypt was directed at one of the Egyptian gods. After leaving Egypt, the Israelites encountered the gods of the sur-rounding nations as they journeyed through the wilderness for forty years. Now they are about to enter Canaan where they will experience polytheistic pagan culture on a level they hadn't before. Canaan boasted a pantheon of gods—one for everything they could think of—sun, moon, rain, thunder, fire, fertility, etc. The Shema was therefore a declaration to the Israelites that the God they worship isn't like the God of the surrounding nations, not the god of this or that, but rather, the one true God of everything: "Hear, O Israel: The Lord our God, the Lord is one! You shall love the Lord your God with all your heart, with all your soul, and with all your strength" (Deuteronomy 6:4, 5). The Shema sets God apart from the surrounding pagan gods and informed Israel's worship of Him. In the midst of a polytheistic culture, the Hebrew people were to know and serve only one true God.

It makes sense then that the Shema became the cardinal Scripture text of the Jewish faith. When the lawyer asked Jesus which is the greatest com-mandment in the law, Jesus pointed him to the Shema (see Matthew 22). The lawyer was no doubt referring to the Ten Commandments, so how is pointing him to the Shema an adequate answer to his question? The answer lies in the fact that by pointing to the Shema, Jesus was referencing the first of the Ten Commandments: "I am the Lord your God, who brought you out of the land of Egypt, out of the house of bondage. You shall have no other gods before Me" (Exodus 20:2, 3). The Shema and the first commandment essentially say the same thing: God is God alone, so worship Him alone with the totality of your being. The Shema sets God apart as the one true God and calls Israel to love (worship) Him with the totality of heart, soul, and strength. The first commandment sets God apart from the gods of Egypt as the one who delivered them and is therefore the only one worthy of their worship. The Ten Commandments begin there because, until we get a handle on God and our relationship with Him, we aren't ready to move on to the remaining nine.

This biblical principle undergirds God's relationship with humanity throughout time—God's imperatives (what He commands) are always preceded by His indicatives (His declaration of who He is and what He has done).

This sets God apart from the gods around us. The reason the gods did not respond during the showdown between Elijah and the prophets of Baal on Mt. Carmel is because they could not respond. The reason Elijah's (our) God responded is because He could—because He can—as He alone is able to. The opening verses of Psalm 90 (believed to be penned by Moses) describe the God we worship: "Lord, You have been our dwelling place in all generations. Before the mountains were brought forth, or ever You had formed the earth and the world, even from everlasting to everlasting, You are God" (Psalm 90:1, 2).

Moses here describes God as timeless (looking backward through generations), Creator of all things, existing before the world began, eternal (looking forward from everlasting to everlasting). God has neither beginning nor end, is self-existent, the existence of everything else in His creation being dependent on Him. This makes Him sovereign over all, omnipotent, and omnipresent, among a host of other attributes.

But like Israel, the twenty-first century church finds itself in the midst of a pluralistic pagan culture in which "spirituality" is actually encouraged and the idea of "god" is acceptable as long as no one god is promoted above the rest. The question therefore is, "What should set the true God apart from the gods of our age and inform our worship of Him?" The defeat of the gods of Baal at Mount Carmel left no doubt as to who the true God was. What sets the true God apart in our New Testament age in which Mount Carmel style showdowns are no longer the norm?

The following verses from Paul's second letter to the Corinthians are helpful in answering this question, an answer that may surprise you:

> The god of this age has blinded the minds of unbelievers, so that they cannot see the light of the gospel that displays the glory of Christ, who is the image of God. For what we preach is not ourselves, but Jesus Christ as Lord, and ourselves as your servants for Jesus' sake. For God, who said, "Let light shine out of darkness," made his light shine in our hearts to give us the light of the knowledge of God's glory displayed in the face of Christ (2 Corinthians 4:4–6, NIV).

Paul essentially says that the central message of his preaching is Jesus, who is the image of God, from whom the light of the gospel shines. The people of the world cannot see this light because the god of this age has blinded their eyes. But on the contrary, this light which the world cannot see shines in our hearts, emanating from the face of Jesus. In other words, Jesus isn't a side note in God's grand metanarrative. He is at the center of it; it all revolves around Him.

Elsewhere Paul reminds us that all that God *is*, is wrapped up in Jesus: "For in Him dwells all the fullness of the Godhead bodily; and you are complete in Him, who is the head of all principality and power" (Colossians 2:9, 10). Therefore, critical to our understanding of God is our understanding of His relationship with His Son, Jesus. Consider the following key passages that elaborate on the relationship between God and His Son:

> God, who at various times and in various ways spoke in time past to the fathers by the prophets, has in these last days spoken to us by His Son, whom He has appointed heir of all things, through whom also He made the worlds; who being the brightness of His glory and the express image of His person, and upholding all things by the word of His power, when He had by Himself purged our sins, sat down at the right hand of the Majesty on high, having become so much better than the angels, as He has by inheritance obtained a more excellent name than they (Hebrews 1:1–4).

> And without controversy great is the mystery of godliness: God was manifested in the flesh, justified in the Spirit, seen by angels, preached

among the Gentiles, believed on in the world, received up in glory
(1 Timothy 3:16).

In the beginning was the Word, and the Word was with God, and the
Word was God. He was in the beginning with God. All things were made
through Him, and without Him nothing was made that was made. In
Him was life, and the life was the light of men. And the light shines in
the darkness, and the darkness did not comprehend it....He was in the
world, and the world was made through Him, and the world did not
know Him. He came to His own, and His own did not receive Him. But
as many as received Him, to them He gave the right to become children
of God, to those who believe in His name: who were born, not of blood,
nor of the will of the flesh, nor of the will of man, but of God. And the
Word became flesh and dwelt among us, and we beheld His glory, the
glory as of the only begotten of the Father, full of grace and truth. John
bore witness of Him and cried out, saying, "This was He of whom I said,
'He who comes after me is preferred before me, for He was before me.'"
And of His fullness we have all received, and grace for grace. For the
law was given through Moses, but grace and truth came through Jesus
Christ. No one has seen God at any time. The only begotten Son, who is
in the bosom of the Father, He has declared Him (John 1:1-5, 10-18).

Obviously, the theological content of these verses is more than can be
unpacked on these pages. However, what we hope is clear is that one can't
have God without Jesus. All of the Old Testament finds its fulfillment in Him.
To know and worship God is to know and worship Jesus. Sound theology (the
study of the nature and attributes of God) is inexorably linked to sound Chris-
tology (a biblical understanding of who Jesus is). This is what keeps orthodoxy (right doctrine) from going off the deep end, separating legalism (I obey;
therefore, I'm accepted) from the gospel (I'm accepted; therefore, I obey). The
gospel is the good news that my relationship with God isn't based on what I
do for God, but on what God in Christ has done for me.

This is important because of the prevailing notion that if a person simply
believes in God—especially if it's the monotheistic God of the Old Testament,
the God of Abraham, Isaac, and Jacob—there's no need to worry about "the
Jesus part." Our theology (our view of God) must reflect a coherent and
unified understanding of the whole scope of Scripture. The God we worship

is the God of both Testaments. Think about it—Handel's Messiah, that classic oratorio on the birth of Christ, is entirely based on passages from the Old Testament. The call of the Shema to love God with the totality of heart, soul and strength points all the way back to creation. Human beings were to walk with God in a relationship of love and unbroken fellowship, but that relationship was forfeited by Adam's disobedience. God's remedy for the sin problem is the gospel, signified as early in Scripture as Genesis 3:15, known in theological terms as the "proto evangelion," Scripture's first reference (or hint) to the good news about Jesus—who is the subject of the masculine pronouns (He and Him) in that verse: "And I will put enmity between you and the woman, and between your seed and her seed; he shall bruise your head, and you shall bruise His heel" (Genesis 3:15). The only one who would perfectly live up to the ideal of the Shama—to love God with the totality of heart, soul and strength—is Jesus, who now lives in us through the Holy Spirit, empowering us to love God in that same way. Jesus was Israel's hope and consolation, the one they languished for and missed by a long shot because they failed to grasp the critical connection between God and Jesus. They failed to understand that all of the Old Testament finds its fulfillment in Him.

So, in our twenty-first century world in which "spirituality" is valued and even encouraged and "the idea of god" is a popular religious phenomenon, Christians must make a rather clear distinction regarding the God we worship, that we worship the God who is revealed in Jesus. This changes everything in "the God-equation"—this is where lines are quickly drawn. This is where Paul's reference to Jesus as a stumbling block (an offense) to many (1 Corinthians 1:23) plays out.

A good illustration is the service at Washington's National Cathedral just days after September 11, 2001. In singing the hymn "A Mighty Fortress Is Our God," the second stanza was conspicuously omitted. That verse references Jesus as the world's ruler and authority, and therefore if sung would have most likely offended the Mullah and others in attendance. It's OK to sing about God. Most world religions boast a god of some kind. But add Jesus to the equation, and the implications change drastically.

Presumably, Larry King, renowned TV interviewer, understood this when asked what question he would ask God if he had an opportunity to interview Him. King is reported to have said he would ask God: "Do You really have a Son?" No doubt, King, who is Jewish, understands that if the

Galilean Carpenter who died on a cross and claimed to have risen from the dead is truly God's only begotten Son (as He is described in the Bible), then Christianity, with its roots in Judaism, isn't just another option among world religions, and everyone must reckon with Jesus' question: "Who do men say that I, the Son of Man, am?" (Matthew 16:13).

A MIGHTY FORTRESS IS OUR GOD
(SECOND STANZA)

Did we in our own strength confide,
Our striving would be losing;
Were not the right Man on our side,
The Man of God's own choosing:
Dost ask who that may be?
Christ Jesus, it is He;
Lord Sabaoth, His Name,
From age to age the same,
And He must win the battle.

— Martin Luther

This brings to mind several assertions made in Tozer's quote at the beginning of this chapter. Our perception of God is the most important thing about us, and is therefore the determining factor of the quality of our worship, because "We tend by a secret law of the soul to move toward our mental image of God." That's why, as Tozer also says, "The history of mankind will probably show that no people has ever risen above its religion, and man's spiritual history will positively demonstrate that no religion has ever been greater than its idea of God."[2]

What, then, is your view of God? Is it informed by a coherent and unified understanding of the whole scope of Scripture? Is your view of God compatible with the picture painted in the Scripture passages quoted earlier in this chapter? Is He the God who has infinitely loved us by coming into this world in human form to rescue lost humanity? He is the Ancient of Days (Daniel 7:9), the God who is making all things new (Revelation 21:5), who surrounds us with songs of deliverance (Psalm 32:7), of whom angels cry, "Holy, holy, holy is the Lord of hosts" (Isaiah 6:3; Revelation 4:8), "the King eternal, immortal, invisible, the God who alone is wise" (1 Timothy 1:17), who now shines the light of the gospel in our hearts, from the face of Jesus (2 Corinthians 4:6). What manner of God is this? What kind of worship does He deserve? Remember, "Worship is pure or base as the worshiper entertains high or low thoughts of God," to quote Tozer again. There's nothing "mamby pamby" about God, to borrow a colloquialism. He reigns in sovereign majesty, and our worship of Him must therefore reflect His power and greatness. Our relationship with Him isn't based on the feats we accomplish for Him, but on the feat He accomplished for us through Jesus. God "raised Him from the dead and seated Him at His right hand in the heavenly places, far above all principality and power and might and dominion, and every name that is named, not only in this age but also in that which is to come. And He put all things under His feet, and gave Him to be head over all things to the church, which is His body, the fullness of Him who fills all in all" (Ephesians 1:20–23). Such is our God. May this be reflected in our worship.

THE PLACE OF JESUS IN THE CHURCH

In his book, *The Reward of Worship: The Joy of Fellowship with a Personal God*, Pastor Jack Hayford devotes several paragraphs to the place of Christ in the church. He begins by saying that "In every generation there are dynamics that press the Church to choose between ever-present points of either commitment or compromise."[3] Hayford lists several such points, but emphasizes that none is more important than the question for which each generation must give account: the place of Christ in the church. Regarding this, Pastor Hayford notes that:

> This question is not decided by councils, though they may affirm beliefs. It is not decided by doctrinal statements, though these may make biblically correct and soundly orthodox statements. Rather it is in the week-to-week lives of pastors and leaders and the worship life of the people who form local congregations that this question of "Who is Jesus and how will I [or we] relate to Him?" is decided. And it is that decision made in the worship place that will determine who Christ's people will be in their homes and the marketplace.[4]

REVIEW QUESTIONS

1. What is the relationship between true worship and an accurate understanding of God's nature and attributes?

2. What is the relationship between God's imperatives and His indicatives?

3. What role does understanding God's relationship with His Son, Jesus, have on our understanding of God and the message of the gospel?

APPLICATION QUESTIONS

1. What is the popular North American view of God's nature and attributes?

2. What type of worship flows out of this view of God's nature and attributes? Why?

3. What is the indicative that precedes "You shall have no other gods before me?" Why is this significant?

4. Who is Jesus to you? How does this impact who you are in your home and in the marketplace?

Endnotes

Scripture quotations are from the *New King James Version*, unless otherwise noted.

1. A. W. Tozer, *The Knowledge of the Holy* (HarperOne, 2009), 1.
2. Ibid.
3. Jack Hayford, *The Reward of Worship: The Joy of Fellowship with a Personal God* (Grand Rapids: Chosen Books, 2005), 81.
4. Ibid., 82.

CHAPTER 20

THE WORSHIP OF HEAVEN

To offer our best worship, we should observe worship at its best, which is taking place in heaven.

After reading this chapter, you will be able to

- identify our model for God-honoring worship;
- list and describe five components of worship as revealed in Revelation 4:1–11;
- identify the worshippers in God's throne room and their characteristics;
- list the two central themes of heavenly worship.

And every creature which is in heaven and on the earth and under the earth and such as are in the sea, and all that are in them, I heard saying:

"Blessing and honor and glory and power
Be to Him who sits on the throne,
And to the Lamb, forever and ever!"

Then the four living creatures said, "Amen!" And the twenty-four elders fell down and worshiped Him who lives forever and ever (Revelation 5:13, 14).

Worship is the most selfless thing Christians can do.

"The worship of heaven is worship at its best, worship that pleases God."
— *Dr. Steven Lawson*

———————————

I t's been said that those serious about honoring God with their best worship should give attention to worship at its best.

Where, then, do we go to observe such worship? A well-known Bible teacher suggests that we should look to heaven where the best worship is taking place, where heavenly hosts worship perfectly and unceasingly. And how grateful we are that twice in Scripture, in Isaiah 6 and in Revelation 4 and 5, the door of heaven is swung open to give mortals a glimpse of such worship—the worship of heaven, worship at its best!

Dr. R. C. Sproul has written a book about worship titled *A Taste of Heaven: Worship in the Light of Eternity*, in which he asserts that worship on earth should be a foretaste of worship that is to come, that worship should be designed to help the worshipper anticipate the worship of eternity. Sproul then poses the million-dollar worship question: "If God Himself were to design worship, what would it look like?"[1] In other words, what would be the essential components of a worship service designed by God himself? What would be its main focus, its tone, its liturgy? Thankfully, as Sproul reminds us, we aren't left without an answer, for Scripture affords us more than one example of such worship.

Therefore, the goal of this chapter is to observe one of these worship scenes. Because of its setting in a new covenant context, we will give our attention to the one described by the apostle John in Revelation 4 and 5. You may be tempted to skip over or scan the verses of this familiar passage, but please don't. Rather, take the time to read it slowly, with open heart and mind, and with senses attuned to the beauty and glory of the worship unfolding in these verses. Use your imagination!

After these things I looked, and behold, a door standing open in heaven. And the first voice which I heard was like a trumpet speaking with me, saying, "Come up here, and I will show you things which must take place after this."

Immediately I was in the Spirit; and behold, a throne set in heaven, and One sat on the throne. And He who sat there was like a jasper and a sardius stone in appearance; and there was a rainbow around the throne, in appearance like an emerald. Around the throne were twenty-four thrones, and on the thrones I saw twenty-four elders sitting, clothed in white robes; and they had crowns of gold on their heads. And from the throne proceeded lightnings, thunderings, and voices. Seven lamps of fire were burning before the throne, which are the seven Spirits of God.

Before the throne there was a sea of glass, like crystal. And in the midst of the throne, and around the throne, were four living creatures full of eyes in front and in back. The first living creature was like a lion, the second living creature like a calf, the third living creature had a face like a man, and the fourth living creature was like a flying eagle. The four living creatures, each having six wings, were full of eyes around and within. And they do not rest day or night, saying:

"Holy, holy, holy,
Lord God Almighty,
Who was and is and is to come!"

Whenever the living creatures give glory and honor and thanks to Him who sits on the throne, who lives forever and ever, the twenty-four elders fall down before Him who sits on the throne and worship Him who lives forever and ever, and cast their crowns before the throne, saying:

"You are worthy, O Lord,
To receive glory and honor and power;
For You created all things,
And by Your will they exist and were created" (Revelation 4:1–11).

This worship scene extends beyond the verses opened before us (through the end of chapter 5), but these first eleven verses set the scene. Let's explore them.

WELCOME TO THE WORSHIP OF HEAVEN

To experience the worship of heaven is to enter another world, another time, another place. That's what happened to the apostle John. We read in this passage that a door stood open in heaven, and a voice like a trumpet issued an invitation to John to "Come up here." This has been called "the divine call to worship"—an invitation to so position ourselves that we are able see God in His glory and fullness.

While we do not anticipate an "other worldly" journey like John experienced, we should be cognizant that when we come before God to worship, we are entering His throne room to pay homage to the King of heaven and earth. Our reverence should not depend on where we find ourselves in worship but on the omnipresence and majesty of the One we worship.

A HIGH VIEW OF GOD

Entering into this "other world," John is "immediately in the Spirit" and begins to observe this heavenly worship service. Note that the service is already in progress; it is unceasing. The setting is a throne room, a place reserved for majesty. At its very center is a throne, a symbol of kingly rule and author-ity, signifying God's absolute sovereignty. This throne is the center of it all; everything revolves around it.

And the throne isn't empty; it is occupied. The One seated on it is "like sardius stone in appearance." There is a rainbow around the throne, a symbol of God's covenant faithfulness, and the rainbow has the "appearance of an emerald." These dazzling colors and precious jewels point to the beauty, radi-ance, and indescribable worth that flow from God's very being, a reflection of His divine attribute called "glory." These verses point to the high view of God in this worship service. In the worship of heaven, God is seen in radiant splendor and is highly exalted. All eyes and attention are fixed on Him—the One who sits on the throne. In pursuing the worship of heaven, we do well to ask ourselves, "Is God the center of our attention and focus on earth?"

And there's more. This heavenly throne room is like nothing ever seen in the palaces and throne rooms of earthly monarchs. The throne is surrounded by twenty-four other thrones. These twenty-four thrones are subordinate, or lesser, thrones, occupied by twenty-four elders, clothed in white robes and with crowns of gold on their heads. Like New Testament elders, they assist the worship of God's people. Their white robes symbolize purity; their golden crowns symbolize the triumphs of God's grace, which they've tasted. Whatever their identity, the elders (?) symbolize authority. This observation is all the more striking as the scene unfolds and they throw themselves before the throne in unabashed worship. This is "throne-centered worship," marked by an overriding sense of the majesty and sovereignty of God.

REVERENCE AND AWE

The verses that follow underscore the deep reverence and fear that adorn the worship of heaven. Flashes of lightning and peals of thunder eliminate the possibility of boredom and distraction. They do this by pointing to the awesome power of God over nature. The very things that elicit great fear and trembling on earth—lightning and thunder—are subject to the greater power of the One on the throne.

Unlike some twenty-first century worship that seeks to remove all sense of reverence and awe, this worship compels the fear of the Lord. As Steven Lawson points out, no one is "high-fiving God and trying to be cool or trendy."[2] The goal of this worship is to deeply impact worshippers—to instill in them the fear of the Lord and awareness of the holy, to the end that they exclaim like Jacob, "How awesome is this place!" (Genesis 28:17, NRSV).

THE HOLINESS OF GOD

But verses 6–8 call attention to yet another dimension of this heavenly worship. There is a sea of glass, like crystal, before the throne. Think about the vast expanse of an ocean, the clarity of glass, and the brightness of crystal, and then combine those thoughts. The saying "Brighter than 10,000 suns" comes to mind.

And what is the purpose or function of the sea of glass? Two possibilities are suggested: 1) It separates the One on the throne from the creatures that surround it. God is holy, separate, set apart, "wholly other." 2) It represents the chaos of evil, stilled and subdued before the throne of God. In either event, the stillness of the sea further amplifies the awe of the worshippers as they approach the throne. To emulate the worship of heaven, our thoughts and worship design—in song selection, order of service, décor—ought to inspire such awe with words and symbols that bring to mind the great holiness and sovereignty of God.

And still there is more to the heavenly vision. In the midst of and around the throne are four living creatures full of eyes in front and behind. These eyes signify constant surveillance. No one approaches the throne without their knowledge. Furthermore, the form of these four creatures—a lion, a calf, a man, and a flying eagle—call to mind the creatures in Ezekiel 10:14, 15. The individual symbolism of each creature has been the basis of much discussion (the lion's strength, the eagle's swiftness, etc.). But more important is their combined symbolism. Many see in them a representation of all living creatures, assembled here to demonstrate the glory due to God from all those He has given life.

Ezekiel helps us by assigning them the name *cherubim*, known in Scripture as exalted angelic beings whose preoccupation is to unceasingly exalt the greatness and glory of God. Revelation 4:8 says that these creatures have three pairs of wings. This mirrors Isaiah's throne room vision in which the creatures cover their faces, because what they see is too glorious to behold, and cover their feet, recognizing heaven's holy ground and their unworthiness to stand there. There's no place in the worship of heaven for pride and selfishness. Rather, we approach the throne in humility, hiding our face from the brightness of God's glory and covering our feet in recognition of the holiness of His presence.

These living creatures have one preoccupation: the unceasing and undiluted worship of the sovereign God. They do not rest day or night! They keep singing. This steadfastness in worship is an invitation to us. We too are called to ceaseless praise and adoration of the One on the throne in every aspect of our lives.

The creatures' song exalts God's holiness: "Holy, holy, holy, is the Lord God almighty." It's been pointed out that holiness is the only attribute of God raised to the "third degree" in Scripture. Dr. R. C. Sproul notes that we're not tempted to repeat other attributes of God in the same sentence (God is just, just, just, for example), but we automatically do so when speaking of

His holiness. Sproul believes it is God's most important attribute because it complements all the others. For example, God's love is holy love, and His justice is holy justice. Holiness is descriptive of God's very person. According to Thomas Brooks, "Holiness in angels and saints is but a quality, but in God it is his essence."[3] Like an onion, if you peel away all the layers if holiness, nothing is left. God is holy, and true worship exalts His holiness. And please note that God's holiness is best observed in His eternal, innate character of love—expressed before time began between Father and Son—and His absolute rejection and separation from evil. Worship that acknowledges God's holiness is worship endued with love for righteousness and abhorrence of evil.

The creatures declare that God is the Almighty, calling to mind the words of the psalmist: "Our God is in heaven; He does whatever He pleases" (Psalm 115:3). All might and power belong to God alone. As humans, we have delegated power and authority. But God has intrinsic power and authority, derived from within Himself.

This puts God and people on two very different planes. We are creatures of earth, bound by time and space, finite. God is infinite—eternal, unchanging. So the living creatures and the twenty-four elders worship Him, casting their crowns at His feet. So overwhelmed by the glory and goodness of God, the elders turn their crowns into instruments of praise and worship, as depicted by these lyrics from this well-known hymn: "Holy, holy, holy! All the saints adore Thee, casting down their golden crowns around the glassy sea."

They acknowledge God as the one who "was, and is, and is to come." This phrase speaks not only to God's eternal existence but also to His determination to redeem and restore His creation. He is the one who is to come. Thus worship becomes, not only a proclamation of what God has done but also a celebration of what He is doing and ultimately what He will do. It is a declaration of the one true God against all pretenders. It is an affirmation that God is returning to earth to set all things right. It is a pronouncement that the time for death, exploitation, oppression, and every form of evil is coming to an end, and that all the forces of darkness and those who align themselves with darkness have an appointed day of eternal destruction. These ought to be features of our worship as well.

As the creatures and elders sing, they cast their crowns before the sovereign God. Recognizing the glory and saving grace of God, they are unwilling to keep the crowns they've been given. This is instructive for us as we each approach God with some level of power, authority, or status. Rather than cling to these things in the presence of God, we are invited to lay them in humble adoration at His feet as unworthy offerings. So they cast their crowns at His feet, singing:

> "You are worthy, O Lord,
> To receive glory and honor and power;
> For You created all things,
> And by Your will they exist and were created" (Revelation 4:11).

Their song points all the way back to God's original purpose in creation. God's ultimate purpose for humanity, the crown jewel of His creation, is His own glory and pleasure in our worship of Him. In other words, we were created for worship. The King James Version renders this, "Thou art worthy, O Lord, to receive glory and honour and power: for thou hast created all things, and for thy pleasure they are and were created." The worship of heaven is worship of God as Creator. As the hymnist declares, when we survey the beauty and grandeur of creation, we are compelled to sing, "My God, how great Thou art!"

But the worship of heaven is more than a celebration of God as Creator. For as we continue into Revelation 5, the worship scene is interrupted by the introduction of a scroll and the question "Who is worthy to open the scroll and to loose its seals?" (Revelation 5:2). The scroll contains God's message for the world, and when no one is found worthy in heaven or earth to open it, John is inconsolable at the prospect of God's Word being silenced. But he is encouraged by one of the elders who notes that the Lion of the tribe of Judah has overcome and is worthy to open the scroll!

Anticipating a Lion, John turns and instead sees a Lamb. This is no ordinary Lamb. It appears to have been slaughtered but is now alive! It has seven horns, representing perfect power, and seven eyes, embodying the seven-fold Spirit of God. This Lamb takes the book from the one on the throne, prompting another chorus of worship.

But where the first chorus centers on God's identity as Creator, this one focuses on His identity as Redeemer:

> "You are worthy to take the scroll,
> And to open its seals;
> For You were slain,

And have redeemed us to God by Your blood
Out of every tribe and tongue and people and nation,
And have made us kings and priests to our God;
And we shall reign on the earth....
Worthy is the Lamb who was slain
To receive power and riches and wisdom,
And strength and honor and glory and blessing!" (Revelation 5:9, 10, 12).

Here we see the full scope of heavenly worship in the recognition of God as both Creator and Redeemer. Here we see the contrast between the worship scenes of Isaiah and Revelation. The heavenly chorus here is singing a "new song" in recognition of the new thing God has done in Christ. God has always been Creator, but in Christ He has become Redeemer of a Creation devastated by sin and death. His beauty and worth is not fully appreciated until He is recognized as both Maker and Re-Maker, Creator and Re-Creator, Lord and Savior.

Worship is incomplete if we neglect either aspect of who God is. Conversely, everything we offer to God in worship is in recognition of Him as either Creator or Redeemer. The two central themes of worship are thus God's identity as Creator and God's identity as Redeemer. Think of it. Is there anything you could express in worship to God that would not ultimately be gratitude for His creating or redeeming you? These then must be the centerpieces of our earthly worship, modeled after the worship of heaven. When we assemble for worship, our focus should remain ever fixed on the biblical drama of creation and redemption. The songs we sing and prayers we pray and sermons we preach should tell this story afresh each time we gather. And this story should shape our very lives.

So this epic worship scene of Revelation 4 and 5 ends where it began—underscoring that worship is the ultimate purpose for which we were created, a fact clearly understood by the participants in the worship of heaven. No wonder the impact of this worship is beyond this world. The focus is God alone—revealed in His fullness as the One upon the throne and the Lamb standing before it. His glory and majesty attract all the attention, and the praises never end: "Then the four living creatures said, 'Amen!' And the twenty-four elders fell down and worshiped Him who lives forever and ever" (Revelation 5:14).

IN SUMMARY

Heaven is where we should look to see worship at its very best. In the worship of heaven, there's a high and exalted view of God. His separateness is also in view: He is holy! The holy God is not brought down to the level of the worshipper. This worship is marked by the fear of the Lord, a deep sense of reverence and awe. It isn't shallow or superficial. Nothing of this heavenly worship scene reflects being cool or trendy.

There is no chance of boredom or distraction either. It is compelling; it gets our attention. There is one focus: the pure and exalted worship of the One seated on the throne and the Lamb who stands before it, calling to mind the themes of creation and redemption. And this worship is unceasing: night and day, forever and ever. The last verses of John Newton's classic song come to mind:

> When we've been there ten thousand years,
> Bright shining as the sun,
> We've no less days to sing God's praise
> Than when we first begun.

> — John Newton

This is worship—worship at its best. This is the worship of heaven.

In many ways, the worship of heaven is unlike anything we've ever experienced. Our goal is to raise the standard of our worship here on earth to match it—to "worship on earth as it is in heaven." May such worship transform us into "the measure of the stature of the fullness of Christ" (Ephesians 4:13). A day is coming when all of human history will narrow down to one thing: the ceaseless worship of the Lamb of glory upon His throne. Until then, may we worship on earth as they worship in heaven!

REVIEW QUESTIONS

1. What should our model be for God-honoring worship? Why?

2. List and describe five components of worship as revealed in Revelation 4:1-11.

3. Who are the worshippers in God's throne room? What are their characteristics?

4. What are the two central themes of worship emphasized in Revelation 4–5?

APPLICATION QUESTIONS

1. How is the worship of heaven similar to today's contemporary worship? How is it different?

2. Every person who steps on stage during a contemporary worship gathering is in some way responsible for leading people in worship. List as many of these roles as you can.

3. What is the model that the throne room gives us for those who would lead others in worship?

4. Consider the different components of your local worship gatherings (announcements, prayer, offering, preaching, etc.). How might each of these be carried out in such a way as to follow the example of the heavenly throne room?

Endnotes

Scripture quotations are from the *New King James Version*, unless otherwise noted.

1. R. C. Sproul, *A Taste of Heaven: Worship in the Light of Eternity* (Colorado Springs: David C. Cook, 2013), 15.
2. Steven Lawson, "Worshiping the Triune God," Light & Heat 2011 National Conference, Ligonier Ministries.
3. Thomas Brooks, *The Complete Works of Thomas Brooks, Ed Volume 4* (Forgotten Books, 2012), 393.

WORSHIP IN SUMMARY

How to conclude a book on a subject as important as worship? A brief summary of its main points seems the best approach, so here goes. We were created for worship, not as a weekly event, but as a way of life. So it was for Adam and Eve in Eden's pristine environment. Worship permeated everything they were and did. The Catechism's classic answer to the question of humanity's chief end—"to glorify God and enjoy Him forever"—was never more fully realized than in their pre-sin lives.

Worship should therefore be our highest priority, personally as believers, and corporately as a church. We're tempted to think that the church's highest priority is evangelism or missions, but the fuel of evangelism and missions, that which energizes believers to take the gospel to the ends of the earth, is worship.[1] A day is coming when evangelism and missions will end, but worship remains throughout eternity.

This assertion about the central place of worship in individual lives and the church finds support in a "worship thread" running throughout Scripture. This is seen from beginning to end, from the altars of Genesis to the praise of the Psalms, to the worship scenes of Revelation. This thread is more prominent in some places, less so in others, but is evident throughout. Worship is central to our lives; it makes sense that it is central to God's Word.

Along the way we find the word worship in some unlikely places. For most, worship is a counter-intuitive response to the news that one has just lost everything, including their ten children. But that was Job's instinctive response to that very report. Worship is what Abraham told his servants he was going to do as he led Isaac further up Mount Moriah to offer him as a sacrifice. For them, worship was not based on external circumstances, but an internal reality, anchored in an abiding relationship with God. Their worship wasn't transactional.

This view of worship inspires us to explore its deeper meaning, to parse its root words in the original Hebrew and Greek languages, and in so doing, to be amazed at how they align across the testaments, calling us away from our stereotypical notions of worship to one in which God is the center and circumference of our lives, honored and adored for who He is.

This then leads to the development of what is called a theology of worship. Theology proper is the study of God's nature and relationship to His creation. The *theology* of anything is the bringing together of its parts and pieces found throughout Scripture to form a cohesive and consistent understanding of it. A theology of worship centers around revelation, recognition and response. From Moses at the burning bush to Isaiah in the throne room, this is the basic pattern we find throughout Scripture, and to the degree this happens, we fulfill the purpose for which we were created, and God gets the glory He deserves.

Closely linked to a theology of worship is observing the worship of God's people throughout Christian history. We don't worship in a vacuum; we are the inheritors of customs and traditions passed down by those before us. God is "doing a new thing," but He wants us to remember what He has done in the past. That's why so much of the Old Testament is given to recalling the history of God's people. God cares deeply about history, because it's "His-story." It teaches us how an unchanging God sovereignly orchestrates the affairs of our changing world, and at the same time is intimately acquainted with the minutest details of our lives. It helps us appreciate our heritage, our present opportunities, and the privilege we have of shaping a vibrant future for those who follow us.

But when all is said and done, it is Jesus' definition of true worship that matters most. What is true worship according to Jesus? His answer to this question is found, of all places, in the account of His encounter with the Samaritan woman. Those who truly worship God are those who do so in spirit and in truth (John 4:23). That is, with the totality of their being—heart, mind and soul. In this exchange, Jesus emphasized substance over style, content over cultural and personal preferences, and right heart attitude over right location. Ordering our worship accordingly can avert conflicts and divisions over worship and save us from the distractions that obscure worship's chief objective—the glory of God.

Distractions include disagreement over musical style and division between the traditional and contemporary camps. Suffice to say, music has the potential to divide because nothing stirs our hearts and emotions quite like it. But for the same reason that music can divide, it can heal hearts and facilitate our worship. In addition, the word "traditional" is a two-sided coin. It can mean rote, ritualistic, void of heart, but it also means classic, time tested, of enduring quality. As for contemporary, it means "with the times." While we're often tempted to pit the two against one another, we need not do so. God cares about both, and so should His people. The task before this generation of the church is to bridge the divide through the selection of music that is balanced and God-honoring, bringing together the best elements of traditional and contemporary forms of worship. There are traditional hymns that have stood the test of time because of their rich theological content, and there are contemporary worship songs that, for the same reason, will not soon go away. Let's sing both. Let's find balance.

Other elements that must be kept in balance are word/truth and spirit/worship. Depending on which one is valued above the other, legalism or fanaticism results, neither of which is of any value to the kingdom. However, Word and Spirit kept in good balance results in the unity and cohesion that should adorn our worship.

Those whose worship is so ordered will give attention to worship's guiding principles. Scripture allows much latitude in worship when it comes to style, culture and personal preferences, but it doesn't leave us without those overarching principles that give boundaries to the practice of worship. In summary, these guiding principles are to: 1) not bind the conscience of another in matters on which the Bible is silent, 2) always consider what is of mutual benefit and edification, and 3) be concerned about how the exercise of our Christian liberty affects those around us.

Getting a handle on such matters, we are better able to navigate difficult areas such as living a life of worship and meaning what we sing. Living a life of worship is no substitute for the acts of worship in adoration and praise, nor vice versa. We must do both. And instead of not singing when the lyrics soar way beyond our present state of mind and heart, we can sing those words as a prayer, a confession, or an expression of intent to raise the standard of our devotion to match the songwriter's pen, to truly love the Lord with the totality of our being.

Loving the Lord that way originates in the Old Testament, where one of the most elaborate patterns of worship is revealed. Each section of the tabernacle and its furnishings foreshadowed an important aspect of worship. Amazingly, the blueprint given to Moses for the construction of the Old Testament tabernacle revealed the pattern for New Testament worship. We therefore conclude that with God there is no Plan B; the worship of His people as New Covenant Christians was always in His heart.

We must therefore be diligent when it comes to designing the weekly worship service. Corporate worship should be dynamic and life-changing, not mediocre and boring. Dynamic worship doesn't just happen, but results from purposeful and prayerful planning.

When we plan prayerfully and come expecting, we are less prone to try to manipulate the Lord's presence, to treat it like a good luck charm, or a genie in a bottle. We can neither manufacture nor manipulate the Lord's presence, nor do any of us have a monopoly on it. The key to experiencing the Lord's presence is making it a matter of the heart.

We make worship a matter of the heart by coming back to the heart of worship. This requires (H) humility, (E) emptying ourselves, (A) aligning our hearts with God's heart, (R) repenting from anything and everything that hinders intimate fellowship with Christ, and being (T) transformed by God as we trust in Him.

Because Jesus reveals the Father, walking close to Him every day, we learn more and more about God's nature and attributes. This is important because what we think about God is the most important thing about us. God doesn't only care that we worship Him; He wants us to worship Him for the right reason. We should worship Him because He is the eternal sovereign God who reveals Himself through His Son: "For it is the God who commanded light to shine out of darkness, who has shone in our hearts to give the light of the knowledge of the glory of God in the face of Jesus Christ"

(2 Corinthians 4:6). In the final analysis, the goal of worship is God's glory, now and forevermore.

We are therefore motivated to offer God our best worship, and to do so, we must observe worship at its best—in heaven. In Scripture, God graciously pulls back the curtains on a few occasions to give us a taste of heaven's worship. Its central focus is the worship of the One upon the throne, revealed fully in Revelation in the Lamb embodying the Spirit. The highest priority of heaven—glorifying the One upon the throne and the Lamb before the throne—beckons us to do the same—to worship on earth as it is in heaven.

We've covered a lot of territory, which is reflective of the broad scope of our subject. But the irony is, we've barely scratched the surface. So continue to sound the depths of this mighty ocean, discovering endless grace and love, the fire and sacrifice of acceptable worship.

Endnote

1. http://www.desiringgod.org/sermons/missions-exists-because-worship-doesnt-a-bethlehem-legacy-inherited-and-bequeathed. Web accessed 3-26-15.

KEEP IT SIMPLE

In character, in manner, in style, in all things, the supreme excellence is simplicity.[1]
Henry Wadsworth Longfellow

A fter we've explored the meaning and priority of worship, after we've parsed worship words and observed the worship of heaven, we must return to the realities of worship on earth. For though we sincerely seek to raise the standard of our worship to match heaven's, for the time being we must worship here on earth. One of the realities of worship on earth is our tendency to trade the simple for the complex. This tendency is humorously illustrated in the story of the investment banker and the fisherman.

> An American investment banker was standing at the pier of a small coastal village in Mexico when a boat with just one fisherman docked. Inside the boat were several large yellowfin tuna. The banker complimented the fisherman on the quality of his fish and asked how long it took to catch them.

> "Only a little while," the fisherman replied. The banker then asked why he didn't stay longer and catch more fish? The fisherman explained that

he had enough to support his family's immediate needs. The banker then asked, "But what do you do with the rest of your time?"

"Well," the fisherman explained, "I sleep late, fish a little, play with my children, take siestas with my wife, stroll into the village each evening where I sip wine, and play guitar with my friends. I have a full and busy life."

The banker scoffed, "I am a Harvard MBA and could help you. You should spend more time fishing, and with the proceeds, buy a bigger boat. With the proceeds from the bigger boat, you could buy several boats, eventually owning a fleet of fishing boats. Instead of selling your catch to a middleman, you would sell directly to the processor, eventually opening your own cannery. You would control the product, processing, and distribution. You would need to leave this small coastal village and move to Mexico City, then LA and eventually New York City, where you will run your expanding enterprise."

Intrigued, the fisherman asked, "How long would that take?" The banker replied, "Fifteen to twenty years."

"And after that?" asked the fisherman. The banker laughed and said, "That's the best part. When the time is right you would announce an IPO, sell your company stock, and become very rich. You would make millions!"

"Millions, then what?" the fisherman asked again.

The banker replied, "Then you would retire, move to a small coastal village where you would sleep late, fish a little, play with your kids, take siestas with your wife, stroll to the village in the evenings where you would sip wine and play your guitar with your friends."[2]

The moral of the story is obvious, but it is stated here for emphasis: More isn't necessarily better; it is possible to spend ourselves in pursuit of what we already have. Achieving the good life usually leaves us empty of the best life—a life of inner peace and simplicity.

Yet the temptation to trade the simple for the complex is ever present. Whether or not the fisherman bought into the banker's investment scheme we aren't told, but it wouldn't be a surprise if he did. Going after such lures—pun intended—is common to our human nature; it's a trait we inherited from our original parents.

Life in the garden was rather simple for Adam and Eve. The first couple lived in a perfect environment and in intimate fellowship with God. To use a Latin phrase, they lived *coram deo*—before the face of God. They related to God transparently, unguarded, without pretense or duplicity. And difficult as it might be to imagine, they had just one command to obey: Do not eat of the forbidden fruit (Genesis 2:16, 17). Pretty simple, wouldn't you say?

Unfortunately, through the deception and craftiness of the serpent, Adam and Eve exchanged God's simple best for Satan's complicated lie. They traded a relationship of trust in God and harmony with each other for a life of confused identity, shame, and blame. No longer comfortable living open-faced before God, they made themselves coverings and hid from Him.

Satan loves when we cover and hide, for it gives him greatest leverage in our lives. The first question asked in Scripture, "Where are you?" (3:9), wasn't seeking information, for God knew where Adam was. It was rather a question of introspection. God wanted Adam to think about where he was and how he got there. Tragically, both he and his wife were in a bad place.

As they covered and hid, the results of the Fall began to be manifest. Suspicion and doubt replaced innocence and trust. All the desires of their heart turned inward. God's image-bearers became self-absorbed: "Make it all about me." They thought it better to receive than give and valued being served over serving others. This evolved into exploitation and murder as early as Genesis 4. More than paradise was lost; the human heart was broken. Sin's corrupting influence was in rapid increase.

These voluminous effects of the Fall make Paul's perspective on what happened in that epic encounter between Eve and the serpent rather instructive. Here's how it reads: "But I fear, lest somehow, as the serpent deceived Eve by his craftiness, so your minds may be corrupted from the simplicity that is in Christ" (2 Corinthians 11:3).

Paul's concern in the opening verses of the chapter before us is the Corinthians' faithfulness to Christ. For an illustration with which to drive his point home, Paul turns to this story of "primary reference," connecting the deception of the serpent with the deception of the false teachers in Corinth, and what Eve lost, with what the Corinthian Christians stood to lose: "the simplicity that is in Christ."

Some Bible translations render this "pure and simple devotion to Christ." The words "pure and simple" are complementary, for in the original Greek *simplicity* conveys the idea of singleness of mind and heart, our affections set solely and singly upon Christ in pure and undiluted devotion.

But in addition, there's a beautiful element of simplicity in the gospel. Jesus, God's best gift to mankind, came wrapped in a simple package. His manifesto, the Sermon on the Mount (Matthew 5–7), is a call to simple faith. The answer to humanity's greatest need is simply Jesus. Not Jesus plus, not complicated formulas, not religious duty, simply Jesus.

This life of simple faith is described by Jesus in His great invitation in Matthew 11:28–30: "Come to Me, all you who labor and are heavy laden, and I will give you rest. Take My yoke upon you and learn from Me, for I am gentle and lowly in heart, and you will find rest for your souls. For My yoke is easy and My burden is light." The words and phrases our Lord uses to describe this life are pregnant with meaning and promise—rest, easy yoke, gentle, lowly of heart, light burden.

But they are directed, not to the world's huddled masses (Emma Lazarus' New Colossus comes to mind), but to a religious people burdened by the demands of the Mosaic Law. To make matters worse, the Pharisees developed a meticulous system by which they added to the Law, increasing everyone's sense of failure and guilt in the process. Speaking of that religious system, the author of Hebrews notes that it was limited in that its sacrifices and ordinances had no effect on the conscience of the worshippers (Hebrews 9:9). Thus it degenerated into a system of external performance, void of a personal relationship with God.

It was to such a people that Jesus issued this invitation, and His offer extends to twenty-first century believers. Burdened by complicated Christianity? This invitation is for you. It is a call to simplicity. It is permission to step off of the spiritual treadmill, freedom from the Christianized rat race that leaves us empty of the life Jesus promised, the life of simple faith.

This discovery opened up a new world for Martin Luther, the sixteenth century German Reformer. His life-changing moment occurred as he contemplated these verses: "For I am not ashamed of the gospel of Christ, for it is the power of God to salvation for everyone who believes, for the Jew first and also for the Greek. For in it the righteousness of God is revealed from faith to faith; as it is written, "The just shall live by faith" (Romans 1:16–17). By his own testimony, it was as though the gates of heaven swung open and the shackles of self-effort with regard to righteousness fell from his feet. He saw in these verses that justification is by faith—trusting in Christ's finished work on the cross. Paul isn't saying that we are saved by the gospel and left to figure out the rest on our own. He is saying there's a power within the gospel itself ("it is the power of God unto salvation"), a power that propels us from beginning to end ("from faith to faith"). The liberating truth changed Luther's life, and subsequently changed Christianity forever.

Speaking of the power of the gospel to change lives, have you ever experienced that personally? Have you ever confessed Jesus as Savior and Lord of your life? It would be reasonable to assume that anyone reading this book is a born-again believer, but such an assumption is unreliable. The Bible's quintessential gospel verse (John 3:16), was spoken to a high ranking religious leader who was neither born again nor understood the meaning of the term. As the saying goes, going to church no more makes one a Christian than being in a garage makes one a car. Perhaps you were raised in the church and religious activity has always been part of your life, but you've never been confronted by the gospel. Whatever your story, if you've never asked Jesus into your heart, believing that without Him you are dead in your trespasses and sins, but that through Him you can have free and full forgiveness, eternal life, pause and do so now. Your life will be forever changed! And, it's that simple.

Therefore, wrapping up this book on worship, the final word is "Keep it simple." The word *simplicity* is part of this book's title because it expresses our ultimate goal: that having explored worship's deeper meaning, readers will respond in simplicity, in pure and simple devotion to Christ.

The opposite would be that readers are able to pontificate about worship without really practicing it. Unlike the false teachers who sought to bring the Galatians under the yoke of Judaism, those in Corinth were given to Greek philosophy and culture, which viewed knowledge as the highest good. Could this be rooted in our original parents eating from the Tree of Knowledge? Is this what the Corinthian brethren were ready to trade—a relationship of love and trust for how much they knew? Is this why they excelled in spiritual activity but lacked in spiritual maturity—the reason they "came behind in no spiritual gifts" (1 Corinthians 1:7 KJV) and were zealous about worship, all the while unable to break free from the influences of their surrounding culture?

What happened in Corinth happens in twenty-first century churches. This is the reality of worship here on earth, the reason we must endeavor not to trade "the simplicity that is in Christ." Descartes' philosophy, "I think, therefore, I am," is common even among Christians, but it is the opposite of faith. Knowledge is never an end in and of itself. It is rather a means to an end. The end goal of all knowledge is that we would stand in awe of our great Creator, lost in wonder, love, and praise.

Purity and simplicity in worship begin on the inside, for these are matters of the heart. Why God accepted Abel's offering and rejected Cain's (Genesis 4) has been the subject of much debate. But Hebrews 11:4 gives a straightforward answer: "By faith Abel offered to God a more excellent sacrifice than Cain." The difference in God's response to their offerings is that Abel gave his "by faith," and Cain did not. The deeper problem was the posture of their hearts toward God. Cain gave an offering because he had to; Abel gave his offering because he got to. Here we're given a glimpse of life at the dawn of human civilization, showing that faith can thrive despite sin's corrupting influence and that Abel's pure and simple devotion to God flowed from his faith.

Reliable research indicates that most Christians don't experience the presence of God in worship, are unable to define worship in a meaningful way, don't consider worship a top priority in their lives, and don't recognize worship as something done for God's benefit. These realities support the need for resources to help believers get a better handle on worship. That is the grand objective of this volume. Having explored worship's deeper meaning, may we now respond in simplicity. Doing so will gradually reverse sin's curse; restore the glory lost at the Fall; turn our desires outward, transforming self-absorption ("make it all about me") into preferring others above ourselves; replace suspicion and doubt with innocence and trust, causing us to live open-faced, unguarded, no covering and hiding, in total transparency before God and one another, being transformed into the very image of Jesus as we gaze continually on Him. As the apostle Paul envisioned, "But we all, with unveiled face, beholding as in a mirror the glory of the Lord, are being trans-formed into the same image from glory to glory…" (2 Corinthians 3:18).

This, dear friends, is not only the hope of the chapters you've just read but also the miracle of worship. May the miracle begin.

Endnotes

Scripture quotations are from the *New King James Version*.

1. Henry Wadsworth Longfellow, *Kavanagh: A Tale* (Boston: Ticknor, Reed & Fields, 1849), 60.
2. Courtney Carver, http://bemorewithless.com/the-story-of-the-mexican-fisherman/ (slightly modified for this use). Web accessed, 1-21-16.

A LITTLE BIT OF WORSHIP ETIQUETTE

Often the word *etiquette* is associated with table manners. But these days etiquette is a big deal, being applied to every aspect of our interaction, including worship.

As you enter the house of God, keep your ears open and your mouth shut. It is evil to make mindless offerings to God (Ecclesiastes 5:1, NLT).

Let all things be done decently and in order (1 Corinthians 14:40).

Make a joyful noise unto the Lord, all ye lands; serve the Lord with gladness, come before his presence with singing.... Enter into his gates with thanksgiving, and into his courts with praise (Psalm 100:1, 2, 4, KJV).

T hese days there are etiquette rules for everything imaginable—from office to business to wedding to funeral to golf, and all things in between. Makes sense, for *Merriam Webster* defines *etiquette* as "the rules indicating the proper and polite way to behave," and as this Amazon resource affirms, that's not limited to the dinner table: *The Etiquette of Kindness—It's Not Just About the Right Fork!* Key the word *etiquette* into an Internet search engine, and more results will pop up than one normally has time to read, including such titles as *Stories of Poor Office Etiquette and Other Inappropriate Behavior* and *The Ultimate Etiquette Violations to Avoid on a Couple's Big Day*. You can even find a compilation of golf etiquette nightmares observed on the course. *Everyday Etiquette: How to Navigate 101 Common and Uncommon Social Situations* and *Etiquette for Idiots and Other Stupid Stories* are among the 26,000 resources featured on Amazon. Indeed, etiquette is a big deal these days, and it applies to every aspect of interaction.

It should therefore not come as a surprise that this vast supply of information on etiquette includes materials on worship. Google shows items dealing with etiquette for worship service, worship team, and church in general. Since worship involves social interaction, since it's "the one thing that affects everything," Christians need to talk about the type of etiquette that should attend and adorn it.

PRE-SERVICE ATMOSPHERE

What happens prior to the service sets the tone for what happens during the service. Understandably, the pre-worship atmosphere is usually marked by the noise and chatter of worshippers who haven't seen each other for a whole week. The goal of this first bit of etiquette advice isn't to squelch that. Worshippers should arrive with the joy of the Lord in their hearts, which will result in some measure of excitement and chatter.

But we must be conscious of the difference between joyful and mindless noise. The word *noise* in Psalm 100 (quoted above) is often misunderstood and misapplied. Understood in its right context, Psalm 100 concludes a series of psalms about the reign of Jehovah. This series of songs pictures Jehovah's assumption of the throne and government of the world. Beginning in Psalm 93, "The Lord reigns, He is clothed with majesty" (v. 1). He is the God of vengeance in 94, a warring king in 95, great and greatly praised with a new song in 96. Psalm 97 describes the effects of His judgments. In 98 He rules with righteousness, and in 99 His kingdom and government are founded upon and governed by holiness. We're now back to Psalm 100, which concludes the series, inviting the whole world ("all ye lands") to witness Jehovah's enthronement. We can be sure that the noise of this ceremony isn't mindless chatter. It is majestic worship fit for a king!

Allow that thought to reshape your thinking, not only about the word noise in this well-known psalm but also about the sound of the atmosphere preceding the worship service. Imagine worshippers preparing to celebrate majesty. Americans aren't nearly as ceremonial as the Brits, whose monarchial structure gives them regular occasion for practicing pomp and circumstance. The closest we come to such fanfare are occasions when our President is announced and the official presidential anthem, "Hail to the Chief," is played. There's usually much noise from the crowd prior to that, but such noise is a reflection of excitement in anticipation of what is to come.

The point is that the atmosphere preceding worship, whether quiet or not, should be marked by the carefulness highlighted in Ecclesiastes 5:1: "As you enter the house of God, keep your ears open and your mouth shut. It is evil to make mindless offerings to God" (NLT). A fish market atmosphere just before the worship service is no way to anticipate the worship of our Lord. Once again, what happens prior to the service sets the tone for what happens during the service, so may the pre-service atmosphere at your church reflect a keen awareness of that reality.

DECENTLY AND IN ORDER

The following is offered to balance the foregoing comments. The saying "A fanatic is anyone who is more excited about Jesus than I am" underscores the tendency of some to write off whatever we're uncomfortable with as unacceptable church conduct, often citing this familiar verse from Paul's pen: "Let all things be done decently and in order" (1 Corinthians 14:40). There are situations that certainly warrant such admonition or reminder, as was the case in the Corinthian congregation to which it was originally written. Paul's purpose was to correct a less than mature approach to the exercise of spiritual gifts. But it should be noted that nowhere in 1 Corinthians 14 does Paul condemn or discourage the exercise of spiritual gifts; he rather encourages it. Therefore, when pointing to this verse, remember its context. This isn't an isolated verse or trump card for whatever makes us uncomfortable. It was written to a specific audience, addressing a specific concern. First Corinthians 14 is instruction on how to do with maturity and discernment what many find unsettling. God wants neither a noisy fanaticism nor a stoic formalism when it comes to worship. He desires worship from the heart that makes us willing to move beyond our boundaries and out of our boxes. As David told his wife, Michal, who considered his exuberant worship undignified, "It was before the Lord that I danced" (2 Samuel 6:21, condensed).

PUNCTUALITY

There's no specific command in Scripture about being on time for church, but there are scriptural principles that underscore the virtue of punctuality. Worshippers will arrive late from time to time for one reason or another, but habitual lateness should cause serious concern.

For one thing, our understanding of the priority of worship should inspire prioritization of time in relation to it. Life is measured in terms of time, talent, and treasure, and none on earth should be better stewards of these assets than the people of God—those called to redeem the time (Ephesians 5:16).

Furthermore, being on time relates to the commitment to excellence to which all believers are called: "Finally, brethren, whatever things are true, whatever things are noble, whatever things are just, whatever things are pure, whatever things are lovely, whatever things are of good report, if there is any virtue and if there is anything praiseworthy—meditate on these things" (Philippians 4:8). Can you think of anything noble, lovely, or of good report about always being late for church?

In addition, settling for a lower standard at church than would be acceptable at work or business cheapens our appreciation for God's grace. We must give our utmost for His highest, even in the stewardship of our time. Ecclesiastes 7:1 says, "A good name is better than precious ointment." Earning a name or reputation for always being late doesn't honor the spirit of this verse.

And last but not least, consider how being late affects those around us. First Corinthians 13:5 says love "does not behave rudely." Frustrating others by making them wait on us, and interrupting a service already in progress by a late arrival is, well, rude.

There's a growing lack of appreciation for punctuality in our culture that is no doubt influencing the church. Don't buy into it. Let us adorn the worship of our Lord with the highest etiquette of time.

> In order for worshippers to be on time, the service must start on time. Delaying the start of the service to accommodate latecomers rewards bad behavior and cultivates the wrong worship culture. Starting on time motivates worshippers to be on time.

APPROPRIATE PLACE FOR APPLAUSE

There's much diversity of thought among Christians regarding the clapping of hands during worship as accompaniment to music, affirmation of the preacher's message, or appreciation for a special rendition. The focus here is the latter: applause in appreciation for special music, etc.

Many sincerely believe that applause is never appropriate in worship because 1) it fosters the spirit of entertainment that is so prevalent in our day, 2) it promotes the idea that what is rendered is performance instead of worship to God, and 3) it detracts from the reverence that is to adorn the worship of God's people.

On the other hand, there are those for whom applause is a genuine expression of appreciation that need not detract from the honor that belongs to God. For such folks, the following etiquette advice is offered: *There are times when applause is in order, and there are times when it is not, and the difference makes or breaks the spirit of worship.*

There are times when the service bulletin will say, "No applause, please" following an item, but that is rare. Knowing when it is appropriate and when it is not is really a matter of discernment, having a keen ear for the most appropriate response. One should be able to tell by the nature of the special music—its message, tone, the reverence it invokes—whether applause will serve only to dilute its impact. For example, a hearty "Amen!" is almost always more appropriate following a solo rendition of "The Lord's Prayer" than is an applause. It is tempting to list other examples, but since an exhaustive list cannot be provided, let's not begin. The bottom line etiquette guideline is that applause isn't always appropriate and that we must carefully determine when it is and when it is not.

> As a rule, during fast-tempo music that lends itself to clapping, the audience should look to the artist for signals as to whether or not they wish to be accompanied with the clapping of hands. Spontaneous and unsolicited hand clapping by an entire congregation during special music can cheapen the value of the item being rendered and can even distract the one rendering the selection.

LENGTH OF THE SERVICE AND SERMON

The Bible says nothing about the appropriate length of a worship service and sermon. But the Bible does call us to exercise temperance (moderation) in all things (1 Corinthians 9:25). On that basis, the length of a service or sermon should be such that it does not weary nor bore worshippers. The incident in Acts 20:7-12, in which Paul preached past midnight until the young man, Eutychus, sank into a deep sleep, fell through a third-story window, and died, is in no way prescriptive for us.

So bear in mind that "The mind can only absorb what the seat can endure." When listeners begin to fidget, it is a good indication that the service has gone on too long and they've stopped listening. And regarding the length of the sermon, here's a good one: "If you haven't struck oil in the first twenty minutes, quit boring."

TURN THE VOLUME DOWN

The last line of the familiar worship chorus "I Love You, Lord" expresses a desire to offer God the kind of worship that brings Him pleasure and delight—worship that is a sweet sound to His ear.

This points to an important element of worship to which musicians, sound operators, and worship leaders are wise to pay close attention. It isn't just important to God that worship be a sweet sound; it's also important to the worshipper. When the volume is so loud that it is jarring to the ears, worship is distracting, and God gets no glory. God created the ear with the capacity to convert audible frequencies into signals that travel to the brain. Numerous studies show the harmful effects of noise pollution in today's environment and its damage on the human ear. These studies go unheeded because our culture is "addicted to loud"—the notion that the louder, the better. We honor our Creator by giving attention to decibel and frequency levels, by commitment to a volume level that is healthy for the ear and enhances worship.

Additional reasons may be cited for giving attention to volume and sound. How about love and concern for those around us, treating them the way we want to be treated? There's also the principle that the voices of worshippers should not be drowned out by the volume of the music or microphone. And very important: We should reach out to those marginalized in the process—seniors, for example, for whom loud music can be a very painful experience because of their hearing devices.

The German reformer Martin Luther is reported to have said, "God gave us five senses with which to worship Him, and it is a sheer ingratitude to worship Him with less." Let's practice the kind of worship etiquette that enhances our capacity to worship God with all five senses, including our hearing.

EMCEEING

Having someone emcee or moderate the worship service is customary in many congregations. To the degree that this practice enhances worship, let it be. But emceeing can be a distraction to worship. In the first place, if there's a detailed order of service in the printed bulletin, there should be no need for emceeing as a standard practice. But if an emcee or moderator is deemed necessary, etiquette guidelines should be carefully followed.

The emcee is not the center of the worship event and should not bog down the service with needless commentary following each item rendered. The Scripture reading in preparation for the sermon is to be exposited by the preacher, not serve as fodder for the emcee's uninspired pre-sermon commentary. In addition, too often the impact of a sermon is intercepted by an emcee who feels the need to re-preach the sermon. The etiquette advice offered earlier regarding the length of the service applies here. In some cases, the length of the service could be cut in half if there were no emcee. The rules of etiquette for emceeing are brevity, clarity, avoidance of redundancy, and the watchword that "This isn't about me."

WHEN TO EXIT

Proper table etiquette includes knowing when and how to excuse oneself from the dining table. Similar principles of etiquette apply regarding when and how to exit a worship service. Except in emergency situations, it is never appropriate to rise from one's seat and walk out of the auditorium while someone is rendering special music or some other item. This is especially true if you are seated in or near the front of the room. From time to time it will be necessary to exit during the sermon or a special, which should be done discreetly. In between segments of the service, or possibly during applause at the end of the praise portion of the service, is usually a good time to exit a worship service. The bottom-line rules are that 1) worshippers should not randomly walk in and out of a worship service; 2) they should choose the most appropriate times at which to do so; and 3) they should do so with the least possible amount of distraction possible.

CONCLUSION

No longer is etiquette concerned only with table manners. It has broadened to many other areas of social interaction, most of which can be informed by how we conduct ourselves at the table. This brings to mind these words of the wise preacher: "He brought me to the banqueting house, and his banner over me was love" (Song of Solomon 2:4). Seated at the Master's table underneath His love banner, may we commit ourselves to the type of worship etiquette that should rightfully adorn our actions and attitudes. God doesn't just want us to worship Him; He cares about how we worship Him. Let us render our utmost for His highest. A little etiquette is good for your church.

Scripture quotations are from the *New King James Version*.

INDEX

ABOUT THE AUTHORS

Whaid Guscott Rose served as President of the General Conference of the Church of God (Seventh Day) from 1997 to 2015. His book *Dream in Progress* and eighteen years of writing for the *Bible Advocate* magazine have shaped that denomination's modern vision. Whaid has served the Church for more than thirty years as a pastor, evangelist, administrator, and author. His passion is to equip the Church to honor God with biblical worship, cultivating a diverse worship culture that attracts all people to the kingdom of God. A graduate of Summit School of Theology, Whaid resides with his wife in Thornton, Colorado. They have two adult children.

Israel Steinmetz serves as Dean of Academic Affairs for LifeSpring School of Ministry. He was a contributing author for the book *This We Believe: Teachings of the Church of God (Seventh Day)* and is a regular contributor to the *Bible Advocate* magazine and the small-church webzine, equipmagazine.org. Israel has served the Church for twenty years as a preacher, teacher, pastor, and author. His passion is to equip the Church to worship in such a way that the world is drawn to the glory of God. A graduate of Christ for the Nations Institute, Regent University, and Nazarene Theological Seminary, Israel resides in San Antonio, Texas, with his wife and seven children.